The Hidden Wealth of Nations

The Hidden Wealth of Nations

The Scourge of Tax Havens

Gabriel Zucman

Translated by
TERESA LAVENDER FAGAN

With a Foreword by
THOMAS PIKETTY

THE UNIVERSITY OF CHICAGO PRESS

Chicago and London

GABRIEL ZUCMAN is assistant professor at the London school of economics

The University of Chicago Press, Chicago 60637
The University of Chicago Press, Ltd., London
© 2015 by The University of Chicago
Foreword © 2015 by Thomas Piketty
All rights reserved. Published 2015.
Printed in the United States of America

24 23 22 21 20 19 18 17 16 15   1 2 3 4 5

ISBN-13: 978-0-226-24542-3 (cloth)
ISBN-13: 978-0-226-24556-0 (e-book)
DOI: 10.7208/chicago/9780226245560.001.0001

Originally published as *La richesse cachée des nations: Enquête sur les paradis fiscaux*
© Editions du Seuil et la République des Idées, 2013

Library of Congress Cataloging-in-Publication Data

Zucman, Gabriel, author.
  [Richesse cachée des nations. English]
  The hidden wealth of nations: the scourge of tax havens / Gabriel Zucman; translated by Teresa Lavender Fagan; with a foreword by Thomas Piketty.
    pages; cm
  Includes bibliographical references and index.
  ISBN 978-0-226-24542-3 (cloth: alk. paper) — ISBN 978-0-226-24556-0 (e-book) 1. Tax havens. 2. Tax evasion. I. Fagan, Teresa Lavender, translator. II. Piketty, Thomas, 1971–, writer of foreword. III. Title.
  HJ2336.Z8313 2015
  336.24'16—dc23   2015019946

♾ This paper meets the requirements of ANSI/NISO Z39.48-1992 (Permanence of Paper).

CONTENTS

Thomas Piketty

If you are interested in inequality, global justice, and the future of democracy, then you should definitely read this book. *The Hidden Wealth of Nations* by Gabriel Zucman is probably the best book that has ever been written on tax havens and what we can do about them. It is nontechnical and lively, and it achieves three different goals in a very concise and efficient manner.

First, it provides a fascinating history of tax havens: how they came into existence in the interwar period, and how they gradually acquired the prominent role that they have today. Next, it offers the most extensive and rigorous quantitative evaluation ever proposed of the global financial significance of tax havens in today's world economy. Finally, and most important, it sets a precise and realistic course of action for change, which has at its core the creation of a worldwide register of financial wealth recording who owns what in stocks and bonds.

Tax havens with their financial opacity are one of the key driving forces behind rising wealth inequality, as well as a major threat to our democratic societies. Why is this so? Quite simply because modern democracies are based on a fundamental social contract: everybody has to pay taxes on a fair and transparent basis, so as to finance access to a number of public goods and services. Of course, there is ample room for disagreement about what "fair" and "transparent" taxation means. But if some of the wealthiest individuals and some of our largest corporations use tax havens and fiscal dissimulation in such a way that they avoid paying taxes almost entirely, then it is our basic social contract that is at stake. If middle-class taxpayers feel that they are paying higher effective tax rates than those at the top of the pyramid, if small and medium-size businesses feel that they are paying more than our largest companies, then there is a serious risk that the very notion of fiscal consent—which is at the core of modern democracies—will fall apart altogether. And if a rising fraction of the population, at the bottom and in the middle of the pyramid, feels that the system is not working for them, and that they are not being well treated by the global economy or by their government, then many might reject the very notion of interclass solidarity and of a fair fiscal and social state. Some might become tempted by nationalist solutions, ethnic divisions, and the politics of hatred.

But what makes Zucman's book so important is that it is not only about abstract principles and dangerous threats: it is about data and solutions. There are systematic inconsistencies in international financial statistics. In particular, there are always more liabilities than financial assets reported by the world's financial centers. By analyzing these statistical anomalies in a systematic and innovative manner, Zucman offers one of the most credible evaluations to date of the global importance of tax havens. According to his benchmark estimate, which should be viewed as a lower bound, around 8% of the world's financial wealth is held in tax havens. In developing and emerging countries, this percentage can be much higher, which makes it even more difficult to build fiscal consent and trust in government and to address situations of extreme inequality. In Africa the share of financial wealth that is held offshore is estimated by Zucman to be around 30%. In Russia and the oil-rich countries of the Middle East (probably the most unequal and explosive region of the entire world), the share of offshore financial wealth appears to be above 50%.

In the United States, the share of offshore wealth certainly seems to be much less than in Africa or in Russia. Offshore personal wealth also appears to play a smaller role in the United States than in European countries, which have been particularly bad at coordinating their policies to fight tax havens. For instance, they had to wait for the US FATCA legislation and the US sanctions against Swiss banks in order to start moving in the direction of automatic information transmission.

It would be a mistake, however, to underestimate the importance of tax havens for the US fiscal system. According to Zucman's conservative estimates, eliminating the US tax revenue losses due to tax havens would be equivalent to an average tax increase of about 20% for all taxpayers within the top 0.1% income group. Also, while the United States may have less of an issue than Europe with offshore personal wealth, they have a bigger problem with corporate tax evasion by multinational companies. Finally, and most important,

Zucman warns us that the FATCA legislation still has a lot of holes in it and that the overall importance of tax havens has continued to rise between 2008 and 2015. We might need much larger sanctions than those that have been implemented so far in order to make real progress. For instance, according to Zucman's computations, the benefits that a country like Switzerland gains from financial opacity are equivalent to the losses that it would suffer from a 30% trade tariff imposed by its three biggest neighbors (Germany, France, and Italy). Of course, we might choose not to apply these sanctions—but then we should not complain when the problem gets bigger and bigger. Global financial opacity is a major challenge for all countries, and there is still a long way to go before we can curb these structural trends.

According to Zucman, the key step should be the creation of a worldwide register of financial wealth, recording who owns what in stocks and bonds. This global financial register would act as a central depository: it would be coordinated by governments and international organizations, allowing national tax administrations to fight tax evasion and to levy taxes on capital-income flows and wealth stocks.

Some might consider the very idea of a central depository as utopian. But it is not. In fact, central depositories for global securities already exist. The problem is that these central depositories are not truly global (they are national or sometimes regional), and most important they are private, not public. Starting in the 1950s and 1960s, securities were gradually dematerialized, and paper titles soon disappeared entirely. This is when modern central depositories were created, simply because there was a need to secure financial transactions and to keep track of who owns what in a computer database (it is difficult to do business if several financial institutions or economic agents in the world claim property rights over the same asset). A number of private financial institutions developed in order to provide this service. The most well-known central depositories are the Depository Trust Company (DTC) in the United States, and Euroclear and Clearstream in Europe. The problem is that these private institutions do not exchange information with governments and tax administrations on a systematic basis. Sometimes they even tend to exacerbate and to benefit from tax evasion and financial opacity (see, for example, the Clearstream scandal in France) rather than to promote transparency.

Zucman's proposal is clear and simple: governments should take control of these central depositories and gradually unify them into a global financial register. The United States, the European Union, Japan, and possibly the IMF should play a leading role in this process, together with the emerging countries in Asia, Latin America, and Africa that are currently losing a lot from tax evasion and capital flight and that are ready to join this cooperative effort. Participation in the global financial register would entail rights and duties, guaranteeing well-protected property rights and financial transactions, in exchange for a commitment to transmit all information that is necessary to identify the actual owners of all assets. This registration system, Zucman argues, should come together with a common minimal registration tax (say, 0.1% of individual net wealth), which could then be supplemented by higher progressive tax rates chosen by national governments (or regional coalitions of national governments).

It is worth noting that the development of centralized registers for real estate and land property titles, together with the creation of inheritance taxes and annual property taxes, played a key role in the building of the modern state and legal systems during the eighteenth and nineteenth centuries. The problem is that these legal and fiscal systems of property registration and taxation were developed at a time when financial assets and liabilities did not play the major role that they do today, and that they were never fully updated for the modern world. In the early twentieth century, income tax systems were created in order to make new forms of wealth creation and income flow—in particular, corporate profits and dividends—contribute to the tax system. One problem that we see today is that it is difficult to properly tax and monitor the income flow generated by an asset if we do not at the same time have a proper registration and taxation system for the stock of assets. This is the problem for modern nations: they still live with a system to register property that was conceived more than two hundred years ago. The good news coming from *The Hidden Wealth of Nations* is that we now understand this problem more clearly, and we know that it can be solved.

Acting against Tax Havens

Tax havens are at the heart of financial, budgetary, and democratic crises. Let's take a look: In the course of the last five years alone in Ireland and Cyprus—two offshore centers with hypertrophic financial systems—banks have gone almost bankrupt, plunging thousands of people into poverty. In the United States, Congress has revealed that one of the largest companies on the planet, Apple, avoided tens of billions in taxes by manipulating the location of its profits. In France, the budget minister had to resign because he had cheated on his taxes for twenty years through hidden accounts. In Spain, the former treasurer of the party in power went to jail after having revealed a hidden system of financing through accounts in Switzerland. Accepting the status quo seems irresponsible.

Each country has the right to choose its forms of taxation. But when Luxembourg offers tailored tax deals to multinational companies, when the British Virgin Islands enables money launderers to create anonymous companies for a penny, when Switzerland keeps the wealth of corrupt elites out of sight in its coffers, they all steal the revenue of foreign nations. And they all win—fees, domestic activity, sometimes great influence on the international stage—while the rest of us lose. In the end, the taxes that are evaded have to be compensated for by higher taxes on the law-abiding, often middle-class households in the United States, Europe, and developing countries. Nothing in the logic of free exchange justifies this theft.

What Is to Be Done?

For some, the battle against tax havens has been viewed as lost from the start. From London to Delaware, from Hong Kong to Zurich, offshore banking centers are essential cogs in the financial machine of capitalism, used by the rich and powerful throughout the world. We can't do anything about them, we're told: some countries will always impose less tax and fewer rules than their neighbors. Money will always find a safe haven: strike here, it will go over there. Capitalism without tax havens is a utopia, and a progressive taxation of income and fortunes is destined to fail, unless we choose the path of protectionism.

For others, the battle has almost been won. Thanks to the determination of governments and to multiple scandals and revelations, tax havens will soon die out. From the harsh words of large countries seeking new solutions ever since the financial crisis, they have all promised to abandon banking secrecy, and multinationals will finally be forced to open their books and pay what they owe. This is the triumph of virtue.

What is missing in this debate is data. Tax evasion by the wealthiest individuals and large corporations can be stopped, but only if we have statistics to measure it, to implement proportional penalties against the countries that facilitate it, and to monitor progress.

It is with this goal in mind that I wrote this book, an economic study of tax havens. I gathered the available sources on the international investments of countries, the balances of payments, the on- and off-balance sheet positions of banks, the wealth and income of nations, the accounts of multinational companies, and the archives of Swiss banks. Some of these statistics had never been used before, and this is the first time that all this information has been collected, confronted, and analyzed with a single objective: to expose the true activities of tax havens and their costs to foreign nations.

Let's say it from the outset: These statistics have many imperfections, and the results of my study are thus in no way definitive. Our system for measuring world financial activity has many weaknesses. But this is no reason not to use it. In spite of any limitations, the available data shed an irrefutable light on the activity of tax havens; and there is no foreseeable progress in ending tax evasion without a quantitative picture of the extent of this fraud. Only on the basis of such an evaluation, however imperfect, will it be possible to impose sanctions and follow any progress in the fight against the scourge of tax havens.

The main conclusion of my investigation is that, despite some progress in curtailing it in recent years, tax evasion is doing just fine. There has, in fact, never been as much wealth in tax havens as today. On a global scale, 8% of the financial wealth of households is held in tax havens. According to the latest available information, in the spring of 2015 foreign wealth held in Switzerland reached $2.3 trillion. Since April 2009, when countries of the G20 held a summit in London and decreed the "end of banking secrecy," the amount of money in Switzerland has increased by 18%. For all the world's tax havens combined, the increase is even higher, close to 25%. And we are only talking about individuals here.

Corporations also use tax havens. Corporate filings show that US companies are shifting profits to Bermuda, Luxembourg, and similar countries on a massive and growing scale. Fifty-five percent of all the foreign profits of US firms are now kept in such havens. Since multinationals usually try to operate within the letter—if not the spirit—of the law, this profit shifting is better described as "tax avoidance" rather than outright fraud. But its cost is enormous—$130 billion a year for US firms alone—and since equity ownership is very concentrated, it essentially benefits only the wealthiest among us.

An Action Plan

To effectively fight offshore tax avoidance and evasion, this book outlines a set of coherent and focused measures.

The first is to create a worldwide register of financial wealth, recording who owns which stocks and bonds. Financial registries already exist, but they are fragmentary and maintained by private companies such as the Depository Trust Company in the United States and the Luxembourg bank Clearstream. The goal would be simply to combine them, to enlarge the field of data, and to transfer ownership of the data to the public. Combined with an automatic exchange of information between the banks of all tax havens and foreign tax authorities, a financial register would deal a fatal blow to financial secrecy.

But how can all tax havens be compelled to cooperate? It is not enough to politely ask them to abandon the financial opacity that allows them to prosper. The second dimension of the plan of action I propose is to levy sanctions proportional to the costs that tax havens impose on other countries. Calls for transparency, new laws, or more bureaucrats are insufficient. Only combined international pressure can truly have an effect, by shifting the incentives of tax havens. One type of possible sanction is trade tariffs. The calculations presented in this book show that France, Germany, and Italy would be able to force Switzerland to disclose all the assets held there by their residents by jointly imposing customs duties of 30% on the goods that they import from Switzerland, because the costs for Switzerland would then be more than the income derived from its banks involved in tax evasion.

Third, we need to rethink the taxation of companies. The fixes recently proposed by the Organisation for Economic Co-operation and Development (OECD) are unlikely to enable much progress. Looking forward, the taxation of multinational firms should derive from their worldwide consolidated profits, and not, as is true today, from their country-by-country profits, because those are routinely manipulated by armies of accountants. A tax on consolidated profits would increase corporate tax revenue by about 20%; this would essentially benefit the large countries of Europe as well as the United States, where the kings of tax dodging—the Googles, Apples, and Amazons—produce and sell the most but often pay little in taxes.

The Symbolic Power of Finance

If we believe most of the commentators, the financial arrangements among tax havens rival one another in their complexity. In the face of such virtuosity, citizens are helpless, nation-states are powerless, even the experts are overpowered. So the general conclusion is that any approach to change is impossible.

In reality, the arrangements made by bankers and accountants, shown in the pages that follow, are often quite simple. Some have been functioning unchanged for close to a century. There have of course been innovations, sometimes esoteric. And we can't deny that there are still aspects of the functioning of tax havens that no one really understands. But, as this book will show, we know more than enough to be able to act against the fraud they perpetuate.

Economists share some of the responsibility for the sense of mystery that still surrounds tax havens. Academics have for too long shown little interest in the subject, with some notable exceptions. But progress has been made within the past ten years, and we may rightfully hope for important advances in the near future. The fact remains that most of the progress in understanding tax havens achieved up to now—remarkable progress in many respects—can be credited not to economists, but to a certain number of pioneering nongovernmental organizations, journalists, political scientists, historians, jurists, and sociologists.

The approach I adopt in this book differs from these earlier ones; it complements them and in no way claims to eclipse them. The originality of my approach is that it is based foremost on statistics. I do not look at individual cases. Though they are indispensable in raising awareness, even scandal, individual case studies are of little help in guiding action. You will not find either oligarchs or African dictators, venal bankers or great money-changers of the city of London here, except in the numbers. This work focuses on an analysis of data and their implications, while respecting their historical context, distinctiveness, and limits.[1]

ONE

A Century of Offshore Finance

O f all the countries involved in offshore wealth management, one has been active longer than any other, and it is still the number-one offshore center today. If we take a close look at this country's banking history, we'll reveal the intricate mechanisms of dissimulation that, starting from its center, have spread out all over the world, and the ingenuity of some bankers in safeguarding financial secrecy and fraud. And while tax havens rarely publish instructive statistics, this country is actually the exception to the rule: there is a remarkable amount of data from the country available, which have received astonishingly little attention. This country, of course, is Switzerland.

The Birth of a Tax Haven

The fabulous destiny of the Swiss financial center began in the 1920s when, in the aftermath of World War I, the main countries involved began to increase taxes on large fortunes.

Throughout the nineteenth century, the greatest European families were able to accumulate wealth by paying little or no taxes. In France, on the eve of the war, a pretax stock dividend of 100 francs was worth 96 francs after taxes. In 1920 the world changed. Public debt exploded, and the state vowed to compensate generously those who had suffered during the war and to pay for the retirement of veterans. That year the top marginal income tax rate rose to 50%; in 1924 it reached 72%. The industry of tax evasion was born.

The industry's birthplaces—Geneva, Zurich, and Basel—enjoyed fundamentally favorable trends that were already in motion. At the beginning of the century, banks had formed a cartel (the Swiss Bankers Association was established in 1912) and were able to make the Swiss government pay relatively high interest rates, which made Swiss banks very profitable.[2] And since 1907, they had benefited from having a last-resort lender, the Swiss National Bank, which could intervene in the event of a crisis and ensure the stability of the entire system. So by the eve of World War I, Switzerland had a financial industry with clear marching orders and a well-developed network of credit establishments. Also, since Switzerland has enjoyed the guarantee of perpetual neutrality since the Congress of Vienna in 1815, it emerged from World War I and the accompanying social upheavals relatively unscathed.

The boom in the tax-evasion industry was also made possible by the transformation of the nature of wealth. In industrialized countries, financial wealth had, since the middle of the nineteenth century, overtaken that of land ownership. In 1920 the holdings of the richest people in the world were

Tax Fraud 101

During the greater part of the twentieth century, it was possible to transport huge amounts of wealth across borders easily, by traveling with one's "pay to bearer" securities. This is no longer true today, because securities aren't tangible objects: they now exist only in electronic form. So to shelter one's money, in lieu of moving suitcases filled with bank notes across borders, the common solution is electronic transfer to offshore accounts.

Let's look at a fictitious example. Michael is CEO of the US company Michael & Co., a firm with 800 employees of which he is the single stockholder. To send, say, $10 million to Switzerland, Michael proceeds in three stages. First, he creates an anonymous shell company incorporated, for example, in the Cayman Islands, where regulations on disclosure of company owners are very limited.* He then opens an account in Geneva under the shell company's name, which takes all of a few hours. Finally, Michael & Co. buys fictitious services from the Cayman shell company (consulting, for example), and, to pay for these services, sends money to the shell company's Swiss account. The transaction generates a paper trail that appears legitimate, and in some cases it actually is. Because companies carry out millions of transfers to Switzerland and other large offshore centers every day—and it is impossible to identify in real time those that are legal (for example, sums paid to true exporters) and those that are not (money evading taxes)—the transaction from Michael & Co. to the shell company's Swiss bank account is unlikely to trigger any money-laundering alarms at the banks.

And Michael wins twice. By paying for fictitious consulting, he first reduces the taxable profits of Michael & Co., and thus the amount of corporate income tax he must pay in the United States. Then, once the money

* Although the Cayman Islands appear often in these kinds of stories, there is evidence that it is even easier to form anonymous companies in Delaware and many OECD countries. See Michael Findley, Daniel Nielson, and Jason Sharman, "Global Shell Games: Testing Money Launderers' and Terrorist Financiers' Access to Shell Companies," working paper, Centre for Governance and Public Policy, Griffith University, 2012.

has arrived in Switzerland, it is invested in global financial markets and generates income—dividends, interest, capital gains. The IRS can tax that income only if Michael self-reports it or if the Swiss bank informs the US authorities. Otherwise, Michael can evade US federal income tax as well.

If Michael wants to use the money, he has two possibilities. For small amounts, he can simply go to an ATM. But for large amounts, he has to be more clever. The most popular technique is what's called "Lombard credit": Michael takes out a loan with the US branch of his Swiss bank, using the money held in Geneva as collateral. So the money stays in Switzerland, still invested in stocks and bonds, while it is also spent in the United States, to buy, for example, a painting by a famous artist or a condominium in Florida.

In sum, the IRS is cheated out of millions—all the taxes owed over time on the income generated by the wealth hidden in Geneva—and Michael can secretly spend his hidden money however he likes.

essentially made up of financial securities: stocks and bonds issued by public authorities or by large private companies. These securities were pieces of paper that resembled large bank notes. Like notes, most of the securities did not bear names, but instead the phrase "pay to bearer": whoever had them in his possession was the legal owner. So there was no need to be registered in a cadastre. Unlike individual notes, stocks and bonds could have an extremely high value, as high as several million dollars today. It was possible to hold a huge fortune anonymously.

If you wanted to keep these paper securities at home under your mattress, you would run the risk of their being stolen, and so owners looked for safe places to keep them. In order to respond to this demand, beginning in the mid-nineteenth century European banks developed a new activity: wealth management. The basic service consisted of providing a secure vault in which depositors could place their stocks and bonds. The bank then took responsibility for collecting the dividends and interest generated by these securities. Once reserved for the richest individuals, in the interwar period these services became accessible to any aspiring capitalist. Swiss banks were present in this marketplace. But—an essential point—they offered an additional service: the possibility of committing tax fraud. The depositors who entrusted their assets to them could avoid declaring the interest and dividends they earned without the risk of being caught, because there was no communication between the Swiss establishments and other countries.

Looking for Lost Securities

Up until the end of the 1990s, the amount of wealth held in Swiss banks was one of the best kept secrets in the world. Archives were kept under lock and key, and banks were under no obligation to publish the details of the assets they were managing. It is important to understand, in fact, that securities deposited by customers have never been included in banks' balance sheets, even now, for a simple reason: those securities don't belong to the banks. Since the financial crisis of 2008–9, the term "off-balance sheet" has acquired a nasty connotation, notably referring to the sometimes complex arrangements that were carried out to remove American mortgage loans from bank books. But one of the off-balance-sheet activities par excellence—coincidentally the oldest and still today one of the most common—is actually of childlike simplicity: holding financial securities for someone else.

If today we are able to know the amount of wealth held in Switzerland during the twentieth century, it is thanks to two international commissions appointed in the second half of the 1990s. The mission of the first—presided over by Paul Volcker, former chairman of the US Federal Reserve—was to identify the dormant accounts belonging to victims of Nazi persecutions and the victims' heirs. For three years, hundreds of experts from large international auditing firms explored the archives of the 254 Swiss banks that had been involved in managing wealth during World War II, producing masses of never-before-seen information—notably, the sum of assets held by each establishment in 1945. The goal of the second commission was to better understand the role played by Switzerland during the war. Presided over by the historian Jean-François Bergier, it also had extensive access to the archives of Swiss banks, which enabled it to establish the sum of securities deposited in the seven largest Swiss establishments during the twentieth century, which, from buyouts to mergers, became the UBS and Credit Suisse of today.

The statistics produced by the two commissions have limitations. Part of the archives had been destroyed; others were kept beyond their reach. But the information gathered by Volcker, Bergier, and their teams is by far the best we have for studying the history of offshore finance. In particular, the data on the assets under custody are of high quality, because, without publishing them, the banks internally kept a detailed accounting of their wealth-management activities, precisely recording the value of the securities that had been entrusted to them, stocks at their market value, and bonds at their face value.

In spite of all this, up to now that information had never been compared to the overall level of European income and wealth in the interwar period, notably due to a lack of statistics on national capital stocks. This is the first contribution of this book: to bring everything together—and the results deserve our attention, for they challenge many of the myths that surround the birth of Switzerland as a tax haven.

The Swiss Big Bang

The first thing we learn is how extraordinary the rise of Swiss banking at the end of World War I was. Between 1920 and 1938, offshore wealth—meaning that belonging to non-Swiss residents—managed by Swiss banks increased more than tenfold in real terms (that is, after adjusting for inflation): it went from around 10 billion in today's Swiss francs to 125 billion on the eve of World War II. This growth contrasts vividly with the stagnation of European wealth in general: due to a whole series of economic, social, and political phenomena, the private wealth of the large European countries was approximately the same in 1938 as it was in 1920.[3] Consequently, the percentage of the total financial wealth that households on the Continent were hiding in Switzerland, fairly negligible before World War I (on the order of 0.5%), increased greatly to reach close to 2.5%.

Who owned all of this wealth? A tenacious legend, maintained since the end of World War II by Zurich bankers, claimed that Swiss banking owed its rise to depositors who were fleeing totalitarian regimes. For proponents of this thesis, the banking secrecy law that was enacted in 1935 had a "humanitarian" aim: it was meant to protect Jews fleeing financial ruin. And so in 1996 the *Economist* wrote that "many Swiss are proud of their banking secrecy law, because it . . . has admirable origins (it was passed in the 1930s to help persecuted Jews protect their savings)."[4]

This myth has been debunked by a great deal of historical research.[5] The Volcker commission identified more than 2.2 million accounts opened by non-Swiss individuals between 1933 and 1945. Out of that total number, around 30,000 (or 1.5%) have been linked, with varying degrees of certainty, to victims of the Holocaust. The data established by Bergier and his team show that it was in the 1920s—and not the 1930s— that the Swiss "big bang" occurred. From 1920 to 1929, assets under custody grew at a yearly rate of 14% on average. From 1930 to 1939, they grew only 1% per year. The two most rapid phases of growth were the years 1921–22 and 1925–27, which immediately followed the years when France began to increase its top tax rates. Swiss banking secrecy laws followed the first massive influx of wealth, and not the reverse.

What does it matter if reality belies the propaganda put out by the bankers? The legend hasn't died—at the very most it has metamorphosed. These days, as is constantly repeated, most customers are fiscally irreproachable and deposit their money in Switzerland only to flee the instability or oppression of their home country. But, as we will see, more than half of the wealth managed by Swiss establishments still today belongs to residents of the European Union (although the share held by developing countries is rising fast), thus making this assertion as fallacious as the preceding one, unless we consider the EU to be a dictatorship.

In the interwar period, the customers of Swiss banks for the most part were French. For example, at Credit Suisse, at that time the largest bank involved in wealth management, 43% of the foreign-owned assets belonged to French residents, only 8% to Spanish or Italian savers, and 4% to Germans.[6] The geographical percentages are imperfect, because the depositors did not always give their true address (instead, some gave that of a Swiss hotel, in which case the funds were recorded as belonging to Swiss residents), but all the other data collected within the framework of the Bergier commission confirm that the highest percentage of capital came from France. On the eve of World War II, the available data suggest that 5% of all the financial wealth of French residents was deposited in Switzerland.

What did hidden wealth look like? For the most part, it was made up of foreign securities: stocks of German industrial companies or American railroads, bonds issued by the French or English government, and so on. Swiss securities occupied a very secondary place, for two reasons: the local capital market was much too small to absorb on its own the mass of wealth that took refuge in Switzerland, and the returns on foreign investments were more attractive—on the order of 5% for securities from North America versus 3% for those from Switzerland. After financial securities, the balance was made up of liquidity (bank deposits such as saving accounts, which appear in banks' balance sheets) and a bit of gold, but foreign stocks and bonds dominated by far. The same is true today, and it is essential to emphasize this point, because it is a source of recurring misunderstanding: for the most part, non-Swiss residents who have accounts in Switzerland *do not invest* in Switzerland—not today, and not in the past. They use their accounts to invest elsewhere, in the United States, Germany, or France; Swiss banks only play the role of intermediary. This is why it is absurd to think that Swiss offshore banking owes its success to the strength of the Swiss franc, to the traditionally low inflation rate prevailing in Switzerland, or to political stability, as its apologists continue to claim. Through their accounts in Zurich or Berne, bank customers from other countries make the same investments as from Paris or Rome: they buy securities denominated in Euros, dollars, or pounds sterling, whose values go up and down depending on devaluations, defaults, bankruptcies, or wars. Whether these bits of paper are held in Switzerland or elsewhere doesn't change anything.

For a customer, the main reason to deposit securities in a Swiss bank is and always has been for tax evasion. A taxpayer who lives in the United States must pay taxes on all his income and all his wealth, regardless of where his securities are deposited; but as long as Swiss banks don't communicate comprehensive and truthful information to foreign governments, he can defraud tax authorities by reporting nothing on his tax return.

The First Threats to Berne

At the end of World War II, wealth management in Switzerland went through a crisis. First, there was a lack of customers. The destruction of the war, the collapse of financial markets, the inflation in the years immediately following the war, and nationalization—altogether these factors annihilated the very large European fortunes that had survived the Great Depression. Private wealth on the Continent reached a historically low level—at scarcely more than a year of national income in France and in Germany versus five years' worth today. Switzerland had not been affected by the war, but the rest of Europe was in ruins. Between 1945 and 1950, the value of hidden wealth decreased, which hadn't happened since 1914.

But above all, for the first time Switzerland found itself under the threat of an international coalition that wanted to do away with banking secrecy. In the spring of 1945, Switzerland, which had compromised a great deal with the Axis Powers during the war, sought the good graces of the victors. Charles de Gaulle, supported by the United States and Great Britain, imposed a condition on this rapprochement: Berne was to help France identify the owners of undeclared wealth. The pressure that was exerted then was all the greater in that a large part of the French assets managed by Swiss banks—around a third of the total, according to accounts at the time—was made up of American securities physically located in the United States (conveniently for the banks and their customers, who could thus buy and sell more quickly). But these assets had been frozen since June 1941 by Uncle Sam, who suspected

Switzerland of being the sock puppet of the Axis countries. To unfreeze them, the United States demanded two declarations: one from Switzerland revealing who really owned the funds; the other from the French tax authorities indicating that the assets had indeed been declared. For Congress, it was out of the question to send billions of dollars via the Marshall Plan without first trying to tax French fortunes hidden in Geneva!

The history of private banking in Switzerland might have stopped there, because the situation was objectively catastrophic. By freezing assets, the United States had a powerful means of pressure. Swiss bankers, with the complicity of the authorities, nevertheless got out of the predicament brilliantly. How? By engaging in a vast enterprise of falsification, which has been documented by the historian Janick Marina Schaufelbuehl.[7] They certified that French assets invested in American securities belonged not to French people but to Swiss citizens or to companies in Panama—a territory where it was already particularly easy to create shell corporations. The US authorities were duped and, with very few exceptions, unfroze the assets on the basis of these false certifications. Boding well for the future, Swiss bankers used this same fraud again in 2005 to enable their customers to escape a new European tax, as we will see in chapter 3.

From the mythology created expressly to justify the banking secrecy law up to large-scale fraud to cover defrauders, everything points to the dishonesty of many Swiss bankers. And so no solution to the problem of tax fraud can be based on their so-called goodwill, as are, however, all the plans recently devised to fight against tax evasion. For example, according to the Rubik agreement with Great Britain, set up in 2013, banks agree—without any checks in place—to collect a tax on the accounts of British customers and to give the proceeds to Her Majesty's Treasury. But history has proven that this approach doesn't work: agreements of this type are destined to fail because banks will always claim to have no, or very few, British customers and will collect essentially no taxes. Therefore, it is essential to break with such logic and no longer rely on goodwill and self-declaration, but on constraints and objective procedures for verification.

The Golden Age of Swiss Banking

By thwarting the first international coalition against banking secrecy at the end of the 1940s, Swiss banks demonstrated their ability to endure. The growth of wealth management quickly resumed, and the three decades of the 1950s, 1960s, and 1970s mark a golden age. Up until the end of the 1960s, the growth rate of assets was comparable to that of the 1920s. In the mid-1970s, according to my estimates, close to 5% of the financial holdings of Europeans was hidden in Swiss bank vaults.

The data series established by the Bergier commission stops in the 1970s, but from there a new vantage point appears from which to follow the development of offshore finance: US Treasury surveys of the holdings of US financial securities by non-American residents. Even today these statistics are still an essential instrument for measuring the weight of tax havens on the world economy.

The first modern survey took place in 1974, and it tells us a great deal: Switzerland, a country that has scarcely more than 0.1% of the world's population, "held" almost a third of all American stocks that belonged to non-Americans, far more than the United Kingdom (15%), Canada (15%), France (7%), or Germany (3%)! To understand these results, you have to realize that the statisticians at the Treasury have no way of knowing who owns US stocks and bonds through Swiss banks. Although they suspect that for the most part they are French or German depositors whose wealth is managed in Geneva or Zurich, they cannot quantify the phenomenon and therefore they credit all assets to Switzerland. Thus the US Treasury surveys reveal not who possesses the world's wealth, but where it is being managed—the geography of tax havens more than that of the actual wealth.

The hegemony of Switzerland over the international wealth-management market of the 1970s can be easily explained. Competition from other tax havens was still almost nonexistent, and even by the mid-1970s London had not yet recovered from the consequences of the war. For rich Europeans who wanted to evade taxes, the situation was the same as it was during the 1920s: the only country that offered the protection of banking secrecy was Switzerland. Bankers took advantage of this to increase the fees they charged, which were fixed by a cartel agreement, Convention IV of the Swiss Bankers Association. Tariffs on foreign securities—established as a percentage of the value of the securities deposited—more than doubled between 1940 and 1983. The profit from tax evasion was thus shared among the defrauders and the banks, and in this monopolistic market, the latter had very little trouble cutting the largest piece of the pie for themselves.

Switzerland also benefited from the first oil crisis of 1973, which made the Mideast Gulf princes rich. For those new investors, having an offshore account is of no tax benefit. The new fortunes are not taxable: not only isn't there any tax on the income from capital in most of the oil-rich countries, but above all in most cases that wealth belongs to the same families who exercise absolute power—including that of imposing taxes—so that it is indistinctly governmental and private, taking the form either of reserves managed by the central bank or of sovereign funds or even family wealth-holding companies, without very clear divisions between these different types of ownership. The reason why petrodollars went to Switzerland in the 1970s rather than the United States is simple: compared to New York, Zurich offered the advantage of anonymity. It was a huge advantage, because the ruling families of the Gulf had every reason to fear that their investments would be closely scrutinized. What could be more arbitrary than their sudden wealth, their ability to buy up companies, land, and real estate everywhere in the world? Swiss bankers would help them exercise this amazing power without attracting too much attention.

In the 1970s the inflow of capital was such that it began to destabilize the Swiss economy. Although nonresidents for the most part owned foreign securities, they were also sometimes eager to invest in Switzerland. That had happened during World War II (when most of the international financial markets were closed), and the scenario was repeated at the time of the collapse of the Bretton Woods system (which put an end to fixed exchange rates for currencies). The problem was that there was so much hidden wealth that if too large a proportion was converted into Swiss francs, the local currency would appreciate dangerously and penalize the entire national economy. To avoid this scenario, in the 1970s the central bank on several occasions imposed negative nominal interest rates on deposits in francs held by nonresidents. The message was clear: foreigners were welcome in Geneva, but only if they were content to buy American or German stocks—not Swiss assets.

The False Competition of New Tax Havens

Beginning in the 1980s, Switzerland was no longer the only player in the game. London was reborn with the liberalization of British financial markets in 1986. New centers of wealth management emerged: Hong Kong, Singapore, Jersey, Luxembourg, and the Bahamas. In all these tax havens, private bankers do the same things as in Geneva: they hold stock and bond portfolios for their foreign customers, collect dividends and interest, provide investment advice as well as other services, such as the possibility of having a current account that earns little or nothing. And, thanks to the limited forms of cooperation with foreign tax authorities, they all offer the same service that is in high demand: the possibility of not paying any taxes on dividends, interest, capital gains, wealth, or inheritances. Consequently, whereas from the 1920s to the 1970s all the wealth of Europeans who wanted to avoid paying

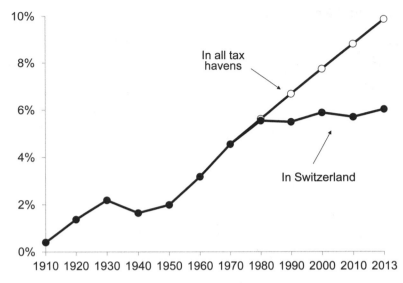

Figure 1: The wealth of Europeans in tax havens (% of the financial holdings of European households).

Source: Bergier and Volker Commissions, Swiss National Bank, and calculations by the author (see the online appendix to chapter 1, www.gabriel-zucman.eu.

taxes went to Switzerland—a few small havens already existed, such as Monaco, but their importance was minimal—since the 1980s the major proportion of the flow of capital has occurred in favor of the new offshore centers in Europe, Asia, and the Caribbean (see fig. 1).

We mustn't exaggerate the competition that these other centers represent for Switzerland, however. In spite of the decline of its share of the market, wealth management in Switzerland continues to prosper. Granted, the rate of growth during the decades of the golden age has disappeared. But the assets managed in Switzerland from the 1980s to the present have continued to increase more quickly than the private financial holdings on the Continent, even if only slightly. According to the latest official statistics, in the spring of 2015 foreign wealth in Switzerland will have reached $2.3 trillion. Around $1.3 trillion belongs to Europeans, or the equivalent of 6% of the financial holdings of EU households. According to my calculations, this is the highest level in history. The death knoll of Swiss banks is thus premature: they have never been as healthy as they are today.

What's more, the competition of new tax havens is in fact only a facade. To view Swiss banks in opposition to the new banking centers in Asia and the Caribbean doesn't make much sense. A large number of the banks domiciled in Singapore or in the Cayman Islands are nothing but branches of Swiss establishments that have opened there to attract new customers. Accounts circulate from Zurich to Hong Kong by a simple game of signatures, depending on attacks against banking secrecy and on treaties signed by Switzerland with foreign countries. Even the historically discreet private banks, a handful of hundred-year-old Swiss establishments where associates are responsible for their own wealth, have branches in Nassau and Singapore.

The Virgin Islands—Switzerland—Luxembourg

Rather than competing with one another, tax havens have in fact had a tendency to specialize in the various stages of wealth management. In the past, Swiss bankers provided all services: carrying out the investment strategy, keeping securities under custody, hiding the true identity of owners by way of the famous numbered accounts. Today only securities custody really remains in their purview. The rest has been moved off-site to other tax havens—Luxembourg, the Virgin Islands, or Panama—all of which function in symbiosis. This is the great organization of international wealth management.

For the most part, investments are no longer carried out from banks. Gone are the days of the capitalism of "small investors" when depositors themselves chose the stocks and bonds they wanted to hold, before transmitting their buying and selling orders to their banker. They have conferred this task to people for whom it is their profession, investment-fund managers. Funds pool the money of the owners and invest it throughout the entire world. This enables them on average to obtain better returns than individual investors, who are then generally content to choose the funds that seem the most promising. But the funds are not located in Switzerland. Most of those in which rich people invest today are domiciled in three other tax havens: Luxembourg, Ireland, and the Cayman Islands.

The classic type of funds, sometimes known as UCITS (Undertakings for Collective Investment in Transferable Securities), has been massively implanted in Luxembourg in the past twenty years. This Grand Duchy, a microstate with a half million inhabitants, is thus the number-two country in the world for the incorporation of mutual funds, after the United States! If you live in Europe, try this instructive experiment: ask your banker to put your savings in a mutual fund and read the prospectus that you are given—there is a fifty-fifty chance it is based in Luxembourg. Hedge funds—funds that carry out all sorts of more-or-less acrobatic investments—are for the most part sheltered in the Cayman Islands, because regulations covering their speculative positions are particularly soft there. As for Ireland, outside of UCITS and hedge funds, it is the chosen land of monetary funds.

Most money managers still work in New York, Paris, or London—close to their clientele—but the funds are subjected to the laws of the tax haven in which they are domiciled. What is the benefit of this maneuver? It enables—completely legally—the avoidance of various taxes created to penalize defrauders. Take the example of a Luxembourg fund that invests in American stocks. By virtue of the tax treaty between the two countries, the United States collects no tax on the dividends that are paid into the fund. In the Grand Duchy, neither the dividends that the fund earns nor those that it distributes to investors are taxed. The situation is identical in Ireland and in the Cayman Islands. Add to this the fact that it costs very little to create funds there, and the success of these three offshore sites is completely explained. In Switzerland, on the contrary, dividends distributed by funds are subjected to a tax of 35%. What is the consequence of this tax, which is intended to discourage tax fraud? Swiss funds have migrated to the Grand Duchy, and from their accounts in Geneva, investors now essentially buy Luxembourg funds.

Switzerland has also left to other tax havens control over the techniques used to hide beneficiaries. Today numbered accounts are forbidden by anti-money-laundering legislation. They have been replaced by trusts, foundations, and shell corporations. In the 1960s, accounts in Switzerland were identified by a series of numbers. Today, through the miracle of financial innovation, they are identified by a series of letters: on bank statements the "account 12345" has become that of "company ABCDE." In all cases, the true owner remains undetectable. In 2012 four scholars attempted to create anonymous companies through 3,700 incorporation agents all over the world: in about a quarter of the cases, they were able to do so without providing any identification document whatsoever.[8]

However, shell corporations are not domiciled in Switzerland, but for the most part in a handful of tax havens where their creation is cheap, rapid, and safe. As for trusts, they are the specialty of the paper-pushers of the British Empire. Today more than 60% of accounts in Switzerland are thus held through the intermediary of shell companies headquartered in the British Virgin Islands, trusts registered in the Cayman Islands, or foundations domiciled in Liechtenstein. An essential point: The Anglo-Saxon trusts do not compete with the opacity services sold by Swiss banks; the two techniques of dissimulation have, on the contrary, become fundamentally intertwined.

Even if Switzerland has lost its hegemony and is henceforth inserted in the great organization of international wealth management, it's important to understand that it remains the heart of the machine for two reasons. First, because the entire chain often starts at its banks: although formally domiciled in the Virgin Islands, the shell corporations are for the most part created in Geneva; and it is Swiss bankers who advise their customers which investment funds to put their money into.

Above all, it is neither the involvement of the Virgin Islands or Luxembourg that enables tax fraud, but that of Switzerland (and comparable offshore private banking centers). Investing in a Grand Duchy fund from an account in Paris—or transferring that account to a shell corporation—does not enable the evasion of French taxes on income or wealth. No matter what one does, fraud originating in French or US banks is impossible, because they fully and truthfully exchange their information with tax authorities. It is only thanks to the lack of effective cooperation of a number of offshore private bankers that ultra-rich individuals are able to illegally evade taxes by not declaring income on their wealth. And although it is not alone, Switzerland is still to this day the number-one place for offshore private banking.

Swiss Banks: $2.3 Trillion

Let's now take a look at a detailed accounting of the wealth held in Switzerland today. Since 1998 we have monthly statistics from the Swiss National Bank (SNB). Until recently, this unique set of data—no other country in the world produces anything similar—had not been studied.[9] According to the latest available information, in the spring of 2015 foreign wealth held in Switzerland reached $2.3 trillion. Since April 2009—the date of the London summit during which the countries of the G20 decreed the "end of banking secrecy"—it has increased by 18%.

Should we be surprised by this insolent trend? Contrary to

what we read everywhere, financial secrecy and opacity are far from dead. Granted, recent policy changes, as we shall see, are making it more difficult for moderately wealthy individuals to use offshore banks to dodge taxes: for them, the era of banking secrecy is coming to an end. Switzerland has agreed to cooperate with the United States to identify some American customers who haven't declared income, and that cooperation should extend to a number of other developed countries by the end of this decade. Swiss bankers are also attempting to get rid of the mattresses stuffed with cash that many Germans or French have inherited, which are too visible and not very profitable. But the decrease of "little accounts" is more than made up for by the strong growth of assets deposited by the ultra-rich, in particular coming from developing countries. For them, impunity is still almost complete, as poor countries are for the most part excluded from the talks to increase international cooperation between offshore banks and foreign authorities.

And $2.3 trillion is probably a low estimate. The SNB data are on the whole of good quality: they cover all of the banks operating in Switzerland—including branches of foreign banks—and all of the wealth that is held in them. But they aren't perfect—no economic statistics are; they are all constructions whose meanings and limitations must be carefully understood. In this instance, the fundamental problem is that statisticians are not looking to identify the true beneficiaries of the wealth. This has two consequences. The first is that some assets attributed to Swiss citizens in reality belong to foreigners. I have attempted to take this problem into account, but there is no completely satisfactory way to

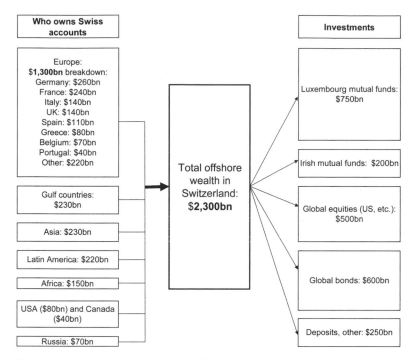

Figure 2: Swiss accounts (spring 2015). In 2015 banks domiciled in Switzerland managed $2.3 trillion belonging to nonresidents. Within this total, $1.3 trillion belonged to Europeans. Forty percent of the wealth managed in Switzerland is placed in mutual funds, principally in Luxembourg.

Source: Swiss National Bank and calculations by the author (see online annex to chapter 1, www.gabriel-zucman.eu).

correct it, and the correction I propose may be insufficient.[10]

More important, 60% of the assets belonging to foreigners are attributed to the British Virgin Islands, Panama, and other territories where shell corporations, trusts, and foundations are domiciled. To know who really owns wealth in Switzerland, we need to make some assumptions about who is behind these shell entities. After examining the available evidence, the assumption I retain is that the wealth held through shell companies belongs to American, British, or German citizens in the same proportion as the directly held wealth does, with a correction to take into account that since 2005 Europeans have had greater incentives to use shell companies and Gulf countries have less incentive to do so.[11] This involves a margin of error, but despite this limitation, the amounts in figure 2 are the best we have available; they are the only ones that are based on the use of a transparent methodology applied to official statistics, covering all Swiss banks, and not on the hearsay or the so-called expertise of groups of advisers or lawyers whose interests are not always clear.

From this figure we can learn two things. First, contrary to a tenacious legend, a bit more than 50% of the total, or around $1.3 trillion, still belongs to Europeans, and not to Russian oligarchs or African dictators. This proves something obvious: Europe is the richest region of the world; the total private wealth on the Continent is more than ten times greater than that of Russia or Africa, and it is not at all surprising that this is reflected in the absolute levels of offshore wealth. The three countries that border Switzerland are logically in the lead— Germany with around $260 billion, France with $240 billion, and Italy with $140 billion.

But the second thing we learn is that the predominant weight of European capital in no way means that tax evasion isn't a problem for Africa or for developing countries in general. Relative to their size, the assets that these countries hold in Switzerland are impressive, and the trend is disturbing. With more than $150 billion in Switzerland—more than the United States has, a country whose GDP is seven times higher—the African continent is the economy most affected by tax evasion. If the current trend is sustained, emerging countries will overtake Europe and North America by the end of the decade. And the consequences of tax fraud are even more serious for developing countries—which lack basic infrastructure and public services such as health care and education—than for rich countries.

What investments do foreigners make from their hidden accounts? In the spring of 2015, out of the total $2.3 trillion held in Switzerland, scarcely $250 billion takes the form of term deposits in Swiss banks. The rest is invested in financial securities: stocks, bonds, and above all mutual funds. Among those funds, Luxembourg holds the lion's share, with around $750 billion.

So today the majority of Swiss bank customers are Europeans, who for the most part control their assets through trusts and shell corporations domiciled in the British Virgin Islands, which provide them with the same level of anonymity as in the time of numbered accounts. Their favorite investment is in Luxembourg funds, on which they pay absolutely no tax.

TWO

The Missing Wealth
of Nations

At the heart of offshore tax evasion is the sinister trio of the Virgin Islands, Luxembourg, and Switzerland. But what is the cost of offshore tax evasion throughout all the tax havens in the world? By failing to tackle tax evasion, how much are governments around the world losing? The available data are too imperfect for an exact, definitive answer, but through a detailed investigation of the available statistics, we can come up with a reliable estimate.

However imperfect, this investigation unveils the extent of tax evasion better than any stolen files or hidden data, which—despite sometimes comprising hundreds of gigabytes—are by nature very incomplete. And since a well-documented estimate is an essential step in calculating how much governments have to gain by imposing penalties on uncooperative tax havens, such an estimate is a concrete advance in the fight against tax evasion.

Eight Percent of the Financial Wealth of Households

To estimate the global cost of offshore tax evasion, we need to know two things: the amount of assets held in tax havens throughout the world, and how much additional taxes would be paid if all this wealth were declared.

Starting with the amount of offshore wealth, my calculations indicate that globally around 8% of households' financial wealth is held in tax havens. What does this mean in concrete terms? The financial wealth of households is the sum of all the bank deposits, portfolios of stocks and bonds, shares in mutual funds, and insurance contracts held by individuals throughout the world, net of any debt. At the beginning of 2014, according to the national balance sheets published by organizations such as the Federal Reserve in the United States and the Office for National Statistics in the United Kingdom, global household financial wealth amounted to about $95.5 trillion. Out of this total, I estimate that 8%, or $7.6 trillion, is held in accounts located in tax havens. This is a large sum. As a point of comparison, the total public debt of Greece—which plays a central role in the current European crisis—is about $350 billion.

As we have seen, the assets held in Switzerland are as high as $2.3 trillion—or close to a third of the total amount of offshore wealth. The rest is located in other tax havens that provide private banking services for high net-worth individuals, the main players being Singapore, Hong Kong, the Bahamas, the Cayman Islands, Luxembourg, and Jersey (see fig. 3). Remember, though, that the distinction between Switzerland and other tax havens doesn't really make much sense: a large part of the assets registered in Singapore or Hong Kong are in reality managed by Swiss banks, sometimes directly from Zurich and Geneva.

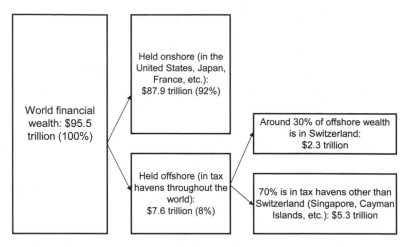

Figure 3: Financial wealth in tax havens (2014). In 2014 on a global scale, households on average owned 8% of their financial wealth through bank accounts in tax havens. One-third of the world's offshore wealth was in Switzerland.

Source: Country balance sheets, SNB, and calculations by the author (see online appendix to chapter 2, www.gabriel-zucman.eu).

Only Switzerland (and to a lesser extent Luxembourg), however, provides direct information on the stocks of offshore fortunes managed by domestic banks. To have a sense of the global amount of assets held in tax havens, one has to use indirect methods.

Here is how I proceeded.[12] I started with the observation—obvious in light of the Swiss case—that wealthy households do not use tax havens to let millions of dollars sleep in savings accounts that earn little or no interest. From their offshore accounts, they essentially make the same investments they do from banks located in London, New York, or Sydney: they buy financial securities—that is, stocks, bonds, and, above all, shares in mutual funds. The money in tax havens doesn't sleep. It is invested in international financial markets.

Now, it so happens that these investments cause anomalies in the international investment positions of countries—the balance sheets that record the assets and liabilities that nations have vis-à-vis one another. The following example shows it in a simple way: let's imagine a British person who holds in her Swiss bank account a portfolio of American securities—for example, stock in Google. What information is recorded in each country's balance sheet? In the United States, a liability: American statisticians see that foreigners hold US equities. In Switzerland, nothing at all, and for a reason: the Swiss statisticians see some Google stock deposited in a Swiss bank, but they see that the stock belongs to a UK resident—and so they are neither assets nor liabilities for Switzerland. In the United Kingdom, nothing is registered, either, but wrongly this time: the Office for National Statistics should record an asset for the United Kingdom, but it can't, because it has no way of knowing that the British person has Google stock in her Geneva account.

As we can see, an anomaly arises—more liabilities than assets will tend to be recorded on a global level. And, in fact, for as far back as statistics go, there is a "hole": if we look at the world balance sheet, more financial securities are recorded as liabilities than as assets, as if planet Earth were in part held by Mars.[13] It is this imbalance that serves as the point of departure for my estimate of the amount of wealth held in tax havens globally.

The Luxembourg Chasm

At this juncture, the essential question is as follows: How can we be sure that the gap between assets and liabilities indeed reflects the money held offshore all over the world, and not other important statistical issues that might have nothing to do with it? The answer is—and this is where the investigation becomes interesting—that the money doesn't evaporate randomly into the ether, but instead follows a precise pattern of tax evasion.

Let's ask the Luxembourg statisticians how much in shares of mutual funds domiciled in the Grand Duchy are in circulation throughout the world. Their response at the beginning of 2015: $3.5 trillion. Now let's look at the shares of Luxembourg funds that are recorded as assets in all countries. In principle, this should be exactly $3.5 trillion, but in fact we find barely $2 trillion recorded. In other words, $1.5 trillion have no identifiable owners in global statistics. This is the big problem. And the same problem appears in the two other places where most of the world's mutual funds are domiciled, Ireland and the Cayman Islands. The funds incorporated in those countries manage trillions. But we don't know who owns them. The bulk of the world's asset/liability imbalance comes out of this.

Now, recall that the preferred investment of Swiss bank account holders is precisely buying into mutual funds, notably in Luxembourg and Ireland. Such investments, by nature, are properly recorded as liabilities (in Luxembourg and Ireland) but nowhere as assets. In other words, when we look at them in detail, the global statistical anomalies are nothing other than the mirror image of the investments made by individuals via their offshore accounts. This is why the global asset/liability imbalance, which amounted to $6.1 trillion in 2014, provides a reasonable estimate of the amount of offshore portfolios owned by households all over the world.

By construction, this method captures only a single type of wealth: financial securities. It doesn't tell us anything, for example, about the amount of regular bank deposits (such as term deposits or commercial deposits) held in places like the Cayman Islands. In the case of Switzerland, such deposits amount to only a tenth of total offshore wealth. Data nonetheless seem to indicate that the amount of bank deposits is relatively larger in other tax havens, notably because most of them are able to provide an interest rate that is a bit higher than in Switzerland. The Bank for International Settlements (BIS) and a number of national central banks provide data suggesting that the amount in individuals' hidden bank deposits was on the order of $1.5 trillion in 2014.

And so the total amount of private offshore wealth reaches $7.6 trillion, $1.5 trillion in the form of more or less "dormant," low-yield bank deposits, and $6.1 trillion invested in stocks, bonds, and mutual funds. This equals a total of 8% of the global financial wealth of households.

Let's be clear: this is not a mathematical truth, but an estimate. There are a number of uncertainties that must be pointed out. First, most of the world's havens do not publish many useful statistics. It's a shame—almost all countries conduct censuses of the wealth managed by domestic financial institutions, but almost none publishes any results on the wealth that belongs to foreigners. The United States, for example, does not disclose the assets held in Florida banks by, say, Latin American residents. The only exception, apart from Switzerland, is Luxembourg, which has recently started releasing information similar to that published by the Swiss National Bank.[14] According to the latest available data, foreign households have $370 billion in the Grand Duchy. This is less than in Switzerland, but Luxembourg—with half a million inhabitants and with an annual income of about $35 billion—is a very small country. In any case, apart from Switzerland and Luxembourg, offshore wealth cannot be directly measured today. Second, the indirect sources of information that I use to bridge this gap—the international investment positions of countries—have known issues, and therefore my estimate involves a margin of error, as is the case with any attempt to capture the unreported economy. It is not possible to say today whether the world's offshore wealth is $7.6 trillion or $7 trillion or $8 trillion: all three figures are just as likely. We can, however, rule out a grand total that would be much less or much more, because that would be inconsistent with the direct information published on the amount and nature of wealth held in Switzerland, as well as with what available country balance sheets—and their inconsistencies—suggest.

$7.6 Trillion or $21 Trillion?

Among the set of alternative estimates that have been produced over the years, James Henry's—which made headlines around the world in the summer of 2012—is perhaps the most widely quoted. I would like to briefly explain why, however, it seems excessive to me. Henry found between $21 and $32 trillion in offshore wealth, or three to four times more than what I find. He gets to the figure of $21 trillion in two stages.[15] He starts with the overall amount of cross-border bank deposits—that is, checking and savings accounts held by German corporations in French banks, by English households in Swiss banks, and so on. According to the figures of the BIS, these deposits amount to a total of around $7 trillion. As we have seen, wealthy individuals do not use tax havens to let their money sleep in low-yield bank accounts; for the most part, they make financial investments. In order to account for them, Henry multiplies the amount of bank deposits by three, relying in this on studies according to which the financial wealth of the rich is generally made up of one-third bank deposits and two-thirds stocks, bonds, and shares in mutual funds: $7 trillion times 3 equals $21 trillion.

This method has the merit of being transparent, of being based on statistics accessible to all, and of enabling a reasoned debate. Nonetheless, it remains quite unsatisfying. First, the figure of $7 trillion greatly overestimates the value of the bank deposits held by households in tax havens. It includes many legitimate corporate bank accounts: German companies sometimes need to have an account in Paris, and hedge funds in the Cayman Islands often keep their cash in London or New York. This may represent spectacular amounts of money, but it has nothing to do with the tax fraud of high net-worth individuals.

The BIS doesn't tell us what percentage of the $7 trillion

in international bank deposits belongs to potential defrauders. This is unfortunate, but it is not a reason to ignore the
problem or assume that 100% of the money belongs to them.
Financial globalization cannot be summed up by tax evasion.
The most rational way to proceed consists of consulting the
data published by the central banks of each country. It so
happens that in most countries, the majority of bank deposits belong to financial companies (like brokers), insurance
companies, investment funds, or nonfinancial companies—
not to individuals, even camouflaged behind trusts or shell
corporations.

As for the portfolios of financial securities held offshore,
the problem is as follows: if, as Henry estimates, these assets
are as high as $14 trillion, then the asset/liability anomalies
should be two times higher than those that we observe in the
data, because all the financial securities held by households
outside their countries of residence are recorded as liabilities
of nations but not as assets. Henry doesn't explain how his estimate can be reconciled with the existing data on this subject.

And the gap between my estimate and Henry's cannot be
explained by trusts and their equivalent. Shell corporations,
foundations, and trusts do not constitute wealth per se; they
are structures used to disconnect wealth from its beneficial
owners. Their worth derives from the financial securities that
are attributed to them. Those securities, from the moment
they are held in offshore accounts, are recorded as liabilities
but not as assets for countries, exactly like those held in their
own name by individuals. They are thus captured by my estimation technique.

An *a Minima* Estimate

Even if the order of grandeur that I propose—8% of the financial holdings of households, or $7.6 trillion in 2014—seems more credible to me than the dozens of trillions that James Henry and others suggest, my estimate is no doubt *a minima*. The method that I use, in fact, excludes a certain amount of wealth.

Out of all financial wealth, it does not take into account the bank notes held in vaults in Switzerland or the Cayman Islands. At the beginning of 2013, the global value of $100 bills in circulation reached $863 billion, and that of €500 bills, $290 billion (more than the annual production of a country like Greece). In both cases, bank notes in circulation have increased greatly since the beginning of the financial crisis. It is well known that most of the high-denomination notes belong either to defrauders, drug traffickers, or all sorts of criminals—how many times have you used a €500 note?

The problem is that it is difficult to know exactly where they are held. In the United States, the best estimates available indicate that around 70% of the $100 bills are found outside the American territory.[16] But we also know that a large percentage is circulating in Argentina and Russia (the two countries that, since the 1990s, have been clamoring the most for Benjamins) rather than in the British Virgin Islands; similarly, a large number of €500 notes are in Spain. Thus it seems unlikely that the liquidity in tax havens goes beyond $400 billion total—on the order of a twentieth of what I estimate to be the total amount of offshore wealth.

Defrauders can also take out life insurance policies from Swiss or Luxembourg establishments. Unlike what happens in private banks, all the money entrusted to insurers is accounted for in their books. In particular, stocks and bonds held in unit-linked life insurance contracts—in which investors can choose the type of investments they want to make and bear all the risk—are legally owned by the insurers, hence appear as assets in the balance sheets of insurance companies, and ultimately in the balance sheets of the countries where the insurers are domiciled. Thus they do not cause any anomaly in the international positions of countries and are excluded from my estimate.

The available data suggest that the wealth entrusted to offshore insurers is still modest today. Unit-linked life insurance contracts are not terribly useful: their main function is to add a layer of opacity between financial wealth and its true owners, a function well fulfilled today by shell corporations, trusts, and foundations, often for much less money. As for regular life insurance policies—in which the insurers guarantee a given amount regardless of the vicissitudes of the financial markets—they are useful but generally offer small returns. In spite of that, the most recent statistics show that Luxembourg life insurance is booming, and who knows? In 2020 the insurers of the Grand Duchy will perhaps serve the same functions as Panamanian shell corporations do today in the great world network of wealth management.

Last, my estimate says nothing about the amount of non-financial wealth in tax havens. This includes yachts registered in the Cayman Islands, as well as works of art, jewelry, and gold stashed in freeports—warehouses that serve as repositories for valuables. Geneva, Luxembourg, and Singapore all have one: in these places, great paintings can be kept and traded tax-free—no customs duty or value-added tax is owed—and anonymously, without ever seeing the light of day. High net-worth individuals also own real estate in foreign countries: islands in the Seychelles, chalets in Gstaad, and so on. Registry data show that a large chunk of London's luxury real estate is held through shell companies, largely domiciled in the British Virgin Islands, a scheme that enables owners to remain anonymous and to exploit tax loopholes. Unfortunately, there is no way yet to estimate the value of such real assets held abroad.

None of the forms of wealth that my estimation process misses are negligible. But my method captures the bulk of offshore wealth, for one simple reason: at the top of wealth distribution—that is, for fortunes of dozens of millions of dollars and more—on average most of the wealth takes the form of financial securities. It is rare that someone invests all of his wealth in a yacht. It is one of the great rules of capitalism that the higher one rises on the ladder of wealth, the greater the share of financial securities in one's portfolio. Corporate equities—the securities that confer ownership of the means of production, which leads to true economic and social power—are especially important at the very top.

In the end, the order of magnitude that I obtain—8% of the financial wealth of households—is likely to be correct, although one might imagine that the true figure, all wealth combined, is 10% or 11%.

The Post-Crisis Dynamic

In a summit held in April 2009, the leaders of the G20 countries declared the "end of bank secrecy." Since then, offshore tax evasion has been high on the policy agenda, and some progress has been made in curbing banking secrecy, as analyzed in the following chapter. Yet six years after the start of this effort, offshore wealth has grown a lot. In Switzerland, foreign holdings are almost at an all-time high; they have increased 18% from April 2009 to early 2015. In Luxembourg, according to the data recently disclosed by the statistical authorities, offshore wealth grew 20% from 2008 to 2012, the latest available data.[17] The growth is stronger in the emerging Asian centers, Singapore and Hong Kong, so that globally, according to my estimate, offshore wealth has increased about 25% from the end of 2008 to the beginning of 2014.

The post-2009 growth reflects both valuation effects—world equity markets have largely recovered from their trough in 2009 and in some places now exceed their 2007 peak—and also net new inflows. In turn, inflows seem to be coming largely from developing countries: as their share of global wealth rises, so, too, does their share of offshore wealth.

While offshore assets are rising, there is evidence that the number of clients is falling, and so the average wealth per client seems to be booming. Since the financial crisis, the main Swiss banks have been refocusing their activities on their "key private banking" clients, those with more than $50 million in assets. The banks know that ultra-high net-worth clients—as they call them—are prospering: a number of establishments publish annual world wealth reports where fortunes of dozens of millions of dollars are described as rising much faster than average and are projected to continue to do so in the future.[18] Bankers adapt to this new trend. Offshore banking is also becoming more sophisticated. Wealthy individuals increasingly use shell companies, trusts, holdings, and foundations as nominal owners of their assets. This is apparent in the Swiss data, which show an ever-rising fraction of wealth held through shell companies, as well as in Luxembourg, where official statistics show that "assets are moving to legal structures such as family wealth-holding companies."[19]

$200 Billion in Lost Tax

The large and rising offshore wealth translates to substantial losses in fiscal revenue. By my estimate, the fraud perpetuated through unreported foreign accounts each year costs about $200 billion to governments throughout the world (see fig. 4). Of course, not all the wealth held offshore evades taxes: some taxpayers duly declare their Swiss or Cayman holdings. But contrary to what Swiss bankers sometimes claim, most offshore accounts are still to this day not declared to tax authorities. I am not speaking here of the accounts of cross-border workers (many French nationals, for instance, work in Luxembourg and have accounts there for this reason), nor of those that many people keep after they have lived abroad. None of those are included in my figure of 8%, and most are declared as they should be. I am speaking of the investment

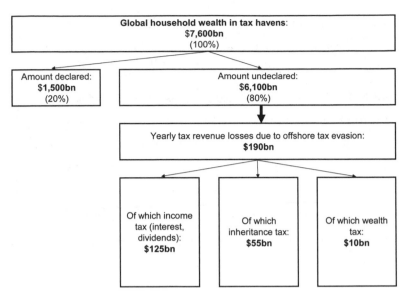

Figure 4: The global cost of offshore tax evasion (2014). In 2014 fraud through unreported offshore accounts cost about $190 billion to governments around the world. *Source:* Calculations by the author (see online appendix to chapter 2, www.gabriel -zucman.eu).

accounts held in countries that cooperate little with foreign authorities, accounts from which one buys stocks or into investment funds.

The key source of information on what fraction of offshore wealth is declared versus being invisible to tax authorities comes, again, from Switzerland. Since 2005 Europeans who earn interest on their Swiss accounts have had a choice: to declare their assets or to maintain their anonymity but be taxed 35% directly by the banks. Now, according to the latest figures published by the Swiss tax authority, only 20% of the assets are voluntarily declared—for the rest, the depositors refuse to reveal their identity. And as we shall see in chapter 3, the 35% tax that was supposed to penalize those who prefer to remain anonymous is easy to avoid, so that at the end of the day about 80% of the wealth held by Europeans in Switzerland seems to still be untaxed. On the assumption of a like basis for other tax havens, this means that $6.1 trillion were not declared globally in 2014.

What is the loss in tax revenue caused by this dissimulation? In most countries, there are no annual wealth taxes: only the dividends, interest, rents, and capital gains that wealth generates are taxable. It is fitting here to debunk another myth that is very widespread, according to which the money held in Switzerland and elsewhere earns little or nothing (hence governments don't lose much). Yes, the return on Treasury bonds is negligible today, but this is not the preferred investment of millionaires—and it is not at all representative of the returns that can be earned on one's wealth.

On a global level, the average return on private capital, all classes of assets included—stocks, bonds, real estate, bank deposits, and so on—was 5% per year during the last fifteen years, and it has only slightly decreased since 1980–90, when it was closer to 6%. This is a real rate—after adjusting for inflation—including interest, dividends, rents, and capital gains. This figure, calculated by using the national accounts data of the leading economists,[20] constitutes a good point of departure to determine the returns on offshore accounts. Using tax havens, defrauders for the most part invest in mutual funds that, in turn, buy a bit of capital throughout the world: Asian stocks, American bonds, London real estate, commodities. Now, the real rate of 5% is consistent with what we know of the rate of returns of the big diversified collective investment schemes sold by asset management firms such as Vanguard. In the course of the last ten years, prudent funds—those that have at least 40% low-risk bonds—have earned on average 6% per year before adjusting for inflation. Those who invest more in international stocks have returned more than 8%. As for hedge funds, reserved for the ultra-rich, their average performance has exceeded 10%.

On the basis of a real return of 5% and taking into account the tax rates in countries around the world, tax evasion on the investment income earned on offshore accounts reached $125 billion in 2014. I am adding to this figure two other forms of wealth-related evasion: tax fraud on inheritances and on the stock of wealth. Around 3% of the assets held in tax havens changes hands each year, and these large estates should on average be taxed at a rate of 32% (with important variations among countries, some having completely given up taxing inheritances). Thus there is the substantial loss of $55 billion per year. Some countries do have annual wealth taxes—such as the solidarity tax on wealth in France—and thus undergo a third loss (on the order of $10 billion). In total, due to tax havens, the loss to government coffers rises to $190 billion per year.

These costs, calculated on the basis of conservative hypotheses, include only one type of fraud, that on wealth and the income that wealth generates. A part of the money that lands in Switzerland and elsewhere comes from activities that are themselves not declared—black-market work, drug trafficking, bribes, false billing, and others. I do not factor in the losses caused by these activities and focus only on those that come out of the dissimulation of wealth, even though the two types of losses cannot be dissociated: the certainty of being able to hide the profits of their crime can only encourage criminals. From a practical point of view, there is unfortunately no way of knowing the origins of funds held offshore and, in particular, of isolating the proportion coming from illegal activities such as drug trafficking from that which comes from the fraud of ultra-high net-worth individuals. Similarly, the losses calculated here do not take into account the costs of the fiscal optimization of multinationals, which pose different problems and will be discussed in chapter 5.

We should also note that these estimates are based on the tax rates currently in force all over the world. Now, governments have tended to cut taxes on capital income, inheritances, and wealth over the course of the last few decades, especially in Europe, in order, precisely, to stop the fleeing of capital to tax havens. Obviously, this hasn't been enough, and so governments are being hit twice: they pay the price of tax fraud, but at the same time bring in less tax on the assets that aren't hidden. My calculations do not take into account this additional cost, which is far from negligible both from the point of view of fiscal revenue itself and from that of equality—the decrease in taxes on capital have above all benefited the wealthiest among us.

Ultimately, the costs calculated here are net of any social benefits accrued through the wealth-management activities of tax havens, for such benefits are almost nonexistent. From the point of view of rich countries, the offshore private banking industry creates no value: establishments domiciled in Switzerland do the same thing as those located in New York, the main difference being that the former sometimes steal from the governments of other countries. If the same standards of financial transparency and effective cooperation applied in offshore havens as in the leading onshore banking centers, there would be no appreciable difference between having an account in Paris or Geneva. Arguably, for developing countries that don't have a well-established banking network, banks in offshore financial centers provide services that would otherwise be inaccessible (such as access to international financial markets); therefore, they are not completely useless.

The Price of Tax Havens

The government revenue loss that I estimate—$200 billion—is the equivalent of about 1% of the total revenues raised by governments worldwide. Should we care about that form of tax evasion? I believe so, for a number of reasons.

First, although 8% of the world's financial wealth (and 1% of government revenue) might seem like relatively low figures, these are global averages that conceal substantial heterogeneity: some economies take a much heavier hit than others. Given the proliferation of tax havens in the territory of the Continent, Europe's economy is the one that pays the highest price in absolute terms. According to my calculations, about $2.6 trillion, or 10% of European wealth, is held offshore, translating into government revenue loss of about $78 billion

Table 1: Offshore wealth and tax evasion: regional estimates (2014)
(Europe and developing countries are hit particularly hard by offshore
tax evasion.)

	Offshore wealth ($ bn)	Share of financial wealth held offshore	Tax revenue loss ($ bn)
Europe	2,600	10%	78
United States	1,200	4%	35
Asia	1,300	4%	34
Latin America	700	22%	21
Africa	500	30%	14
Canada	300	9%	6
Russia	200	52%	1
Gulf countries	800	57%	0
Total	7,600	8.0%	190

Source: Calculations by the author (see online appendix to chapter 2, www.gabriel-zucman.eu).

in 2014. But in relative terms, it is developing countries that are most affected: for them the fraction of wealth held abroad is considerable, ranging from 20% to 30% in many African and Latin American countries, to as much as 50% in Russia.

Even where offshore wealth reaches less extreme proportions, it is important to note that this form of evasion benefits almost entirely the wealthiest. In the United States, according to my estimate, offshore evasion costs about $35 billion annually. For comparison, the top 0.1% highest income earners paid about $200 billion in federal income taxes in 2014. Assuming that all unrecorded offshore wealth belongs to the top 0.1%, eradicating offshore evasion would thus raise as much revenue as increasing the top 0.1%'s federal income tax bill by close to 18%.

Public Debt, Hidden Wealth

Collecting more tax is certainty not a goal in itself, especially in countries like France, where taxes are already high. If the struggle against fraud is essential, it is because it would make it possible to lower the tax that is imposed on the vast majority of taxpayers—those who do not have wealth to hide and benefit little or not at all by tax loopholes—and would contribute to reestablishing the balance of public finances, with the added benefits of more growth and social justice.

This issue is again particularly relevant for Europe, where many countries are entrapped in the spiral of austerity. Growth has tended to be anemic since the financial crisis of 2008–9, pushing the ratio of public debt to GDP up; in response, governments have tended to slash spending, which has depressed demand, further reducing growth and increasing debt. Battling offshore tax havens would help reverse this deadly spiral. Greece wouldn't have to impose as much austerity on its citizens to satisfy the demands of European authorities if the government could bring its elites to heel. France would have more leeway to stimulate its economy without upsetting the Germans.

Imagine, for instance, that French hidden wealth suddenly becomes taxable. Any form of amnesty for defrauders would be out of the question, as it would be unacceptable for the law not to be applied to the rich and powerful. Ideally, the tax authority should treat each case on its own merits, establish fines according to legislation (in function of the amount of tax owed, the duration of the fraud, et cetera) and carry out any necessary legal actions. In many cases, this might result in total levies (past taxes owed, penalties, fines) of 100% or close to 100% of the total amount of wealth previously hidden. Spain has recently adopted a law applying sanctions potentially even higher than 100% of hidden assets—in addition to losing their accounts, the defrauders could have their house seized, for example.

To expedite the process, when the administration is certain that hidden money did not come from illegal activities and is not an active form of tax evasion (for example, in the case of inherited accounts), it might offer to ignore the exact amount of evaded tax, not publicize the identities of the defrauders, but in exchange tax the undeclared assets at 100%. If most cases were settled in this way, France could recover around €300 billion—15% of GDP—immediately. In the current context, it seems appropriate that the government would decide to allocate all of the sums collected in this way to reducing the public debt. The immediate benefit would be doubled, since interest expense on the debt would also be reduced. The economic models we currently have suggest that the private wealth taxed away by the state would ultimately be re-created (thanks to savings), thereby generating supplemental capital-income tax and inheritance tax revenue in the future, which could serve to lower other taxes, such as the tax on the income of the middle classes or the VAT.

THREE

Mistakes

There are concrete solutions to putting an end to offshore personal tax evasion. But before we explore these, we should discover the lessons of past attempts. Up to now, such attempts have all resulted in failure for two main reasons: a lack of constraints and a lack of verification. Some recent initiatives—such as the Foreign Account Tax Compliance Act in the United States and similar laws abroad—are very promising, but unless we learn from the past, these initiatives will fail to change things.

And Automatic Exchange Was Born . . .

The first policies to fight against tax havens go back to the belle époque, at the beginning of the twentieth century, when the modern social state and progressive taxation began to develop. For reformers, the question of progress and that of the fight against fraud were one and the same. When tax evasion is possible for the wealthy, there can be no consent for taxes. And without taxes, there are no resources to finance schools, hospitals, and roads; nor to redistribute wealth, even slightly, to ensure the equality of opportunities.

One hundred years ago, there was no one in France who understood this better than Joseph Caillaux. In 1908, when he was minister of finance, he waged two battles of great modernity on the front lines: the battle for the creation of a unified and progressive tax on income, on the one hand (it would come to pass in 1914), and that against tax havens, on the other.

The atmosphere was electric. A few years earlier, in 1901, France had made the inheritance tax that had existed since the Revolution progressive. The rates of the new tax were modest: a maximum of 5% for the largest inheritances from parents to children, as opposed to 1% regardless of the amount inherited that had existed up to then. But the reform provoked an outcry among the conservatives, for whom taxing inherited wealth at 5% was a violation of private property. They went to great lengths to contain what Paul Leroy-Beaulieu called the "virus of progression." Their argument? Not only did the progressive taxation of people threaten the foundations of society, but it would give new life to an impulse for fraud. Although it is impossible to know if that concern was legitimate, the fear of tax evasion delayed the adoption of the income tax, encouraging reformers to look for new ways to secure tax compliance.

The law of 1901 introduced a first, revolutionary anti-fraud mechanism: the automatic exchange of information between banks and the tax authorities. Up until then, in order to take possession of an account after the death of its owner, an individual had only to present a statement from his notary designating him as the rightful owner. Heirs, of course, had to pay inheritance tax, but there were no controls over this. By virtue of the new law, banks were henceforth obligated to inform the administration of all inheritances of which they were aware. The law thus asserted that banking secrecy did not apply to questions of taxation. And, what was more important, cooperation between the banks and the public authorities was to be automatic and not upon the request of the authorities.

The automatic exchange of information that was codified at the time did, however, have limits: it was only national. Only French banks were implicated. And for decades some of the wealthiest people in France were already using private English, Dutch, or Swiss banks to manage their assets. In these offshore institutions, inheritances could still be transferred without being taxed.

Caillaux quickly tackled the problem. On March 12, 1908, he submitted a "proposed law intended to prevent fraud in matters of inheritance tax," aimed at tax evasion through foreign banks.[21] The proposed law stated that henceforth banks would be obligated to ensure that their clients indeed paid their inheritance tax by automatically including a statement on notary documents. Defrauders were subject to a fine equal to 25% of the hidden funds.

The law, however, was not passed. Conservatives, who were in the majority in the Sénat, despised Caillaux—it was a hatred, moreover, that would push his wife, Henriette, in 1914 to assassinate the director of the right-wing newspaper *Le Figaro* following a final press campaign. Without having the majority in Parliament, Caillaux sent his emissaries to negotiate accords of fiscal cooperation directly with the great European powers. A treaty was quickly signed with England. It functioned as follows: in the United Kingdom, the estate of every deceased person is conferred to trustees, and the heirs can take possession of their inheritance only after a hearing in front of a special probate court. By virtue of the Franco-English agreement, that court could henceforth not rule until it had informed the French administration of the amount inherited by a French taxpayer. In front of the deputies, Caillaux expressed pride in this accord, of which he said he had already "experienced the impact" (unfortunately, he didn't provide any figures).

That was in 1908, and the first international treaty for an automatic exchange of information was born.

The Masquerade of On-Demand Exchanges

A century later, we must mourn the time that has been lost. In 2009, mandated by the G20 countries to fight against international tax fraud, the OECD instituted a particularly weak form of mutual help, an on-demand exchange of information.

To obtain banking information from a tax haven, a country such as the United Kingdom must first have well-founded suspicions of fraud against one of its residents, which in practice is almost impossible to prove. In the absence of any evidence, tax havens do not have to cooperate. One hundred years earlier, no one would have envisioned tackling the problem in such a simplistic way. The OECD, however, declared that the era of banking secrecy was over; for then French president Sarkozy, it was the "end of tax havens."

When we take stock of this policy today, it is disturbing. Tax havens have signed hundreds of treaties for the on-demand exchange of information. Yet through these treaties, countries like the United Kingdom gather only a few dozen pieces of information each year, whereas hundreds of thousands of UK residents have foreign bank accounts. In spite of the resounding declarations of progress, defrauders go about their business with almost complete impunity. The only risk they run is if the tax authorities get their hands on stolen files or happen to obtain information on undeclared accounts—for example, through clandestine reports—the only methods capable of feeding a valid demand for mutual help. The supreme irony is that a policy of on-demand exchange can thus function only by exploiting information obtained on the edge of legality.

And so it is not surprising that this strategy has had little effect on fraud. Between 2009 and early 2015, as we saw in chapter 1, the total amount of foreign wealth managed in Switzerland has increased by 18%. According to my estimates, on a global level—all tax havens combined—the increase has been even greater, on the order of 25%. There is some evidence that voluntary declarations have increased—20% of the funds held by Europeans in Switzerland are now being reported to tax authorities, against less than 10% before the financial crisis—but most of the wealth in Switzerland continues to be hidden.

Devoid of meaning, the policy of on-demand exchange in fact turned out to be counterproductive. At the April 2009 summit, the G20 countries had decided that tax havens should each sign at least 12 treaties to be compliant and to be removed from the blacklist of uncooperative states. Why 12 and not 27 or 143? No one knows. Because of this arbitrarily low threshold, the network of treaties in effect today is full of holes. Nothing could be easier than to send one's money to a tax haven that is not tied by an agreement with the country in which one lives. According to the available data, the small minority of defrauders who reacted to the G20 policy did not do so by bringing back their assets to their country, but by sending them to the least cooperative places, those that signed the fewest treaties for information exchange with foreign countries.[22] Between 2009 and 2013, Singapore thus gained the equivalent of 4% of the global amount of offshore banking deposits, Hong Kong, 5%; Jersey, on the other hand, lost 4%.

For the most part, such movement represents a simple shell game: most establishments domiciled in the Anglo-Norman islands and in Singapore are branches of the same multinational private wealth-management groups. The money stays inside the same banks, but it chooses the most advantageous laws (or rather, non-laws)—and those of the tax havens in Asia are today the most protective, in particular because American pressure is much weaker there than in Switzerland. Transfers are made with the click of a mouse—there is no need to carry suitcases full of bank notes across the globe. The more money that goes in, the more the strategy of the aggressive tax havens is validated. This episode teaches us an important lesson: a partial fight against tax havens is actually counterproductive because it increases the incentive of the remaining havens not to cooperate; to be effective, a fight against tax evasion has to be truly global.

Perhaps the most spectacular illustration of the pitfalls of on-demand information exchange comes from France, from what is known there as the Cahuzac affair. Jérôme Cahuzac, a member of the Socialist Party, was appointed by President François Hollande as minister of the budget in May 2012. In this respect, he was the very person in charge of fighting tax evasion at the highest level in the French administration. Yet at the end of 2012, an online investigative newspaper, *Mediapart*, published a recording (dating from the early 2000s) in which Cahuzac is heard mentioning his hidden account in the Swiss bank UBS. A political scandal ensued: Did Cahuzac actually possess undeclared assets? To find out, the French authorities used the cooperation agreement signed with Switzerland in 2009. The response of the Swiss authorities was negative. The on-demand exchange treaty, in other words, laundered the launderer. An independent judicial inquiry a few weeks later would discover that in fact the hidden account had been transferred to Singapore, leading to the minister's resignation.

Foreign Account Tax Compliance Act

Fortunately, at the time the OECD went for on-demand information exchange, the United States started exploring an alternative, more meaningful strategy. In 2010 Congress passed and President Obama signed into law the Foreign Account Tax Compliance Act. FATCA imposes an automatic exchange of data between foreign banks and the Internal Revenue Service. Financial institutions throughout the world must identify who, among their clients, are American citizens and inform the IRS what each person holds in his or her account and the income earned on it. There is no requirement for prior suspicion: the exchange of data has to be automatic, every year, just like US banks automatically send information to the IRS to ensure that taxes on interest income, dividends, and capital gains are properly paid.

The Foreign Account Tax Compliance Act has been criticized on a number of grounds. FATCA, some argue, asserts US government power over foreign-based financial firms; it invades privacy; and the US government does not require reciprocal reporting to other countries regarding assets held by foreign households in US banks. Above all, it creates difficulties for ordinary Americans overseas because foreign banks may choose simply not to offer or to sharply limit accounts to Americans rather than deal with the FATCA requirements. Some of these issues have merits. In particular, there is a real risk that FATCA will impose substantial administrative burdens on many law-abiding US taxpayers and the financial institutions that serve them, while at the same time failing to catch the most aggressive tax dodgers. Notwithstanding, FATCA has been the starting point toward changing the ground rules that previously governed offshore banking.

The key provision of FATCA is that foreign banks refusing to disclose accounts held by US taxpayers face clearly defined economic sanctions: a 30% tax on all dividends and interest income paid to them by the United States. That threat has proven effective in securing the (formal) cooperation of most of the world's tax havens and financial institutions (whether real cooperation will ensue is less clear, as we shall see). Some large countries were initially skeptical—the Chinese authorities publicly criticized the American law, before halfheartedly praising automatic exchanges in the summer of 2013. And there are still today some cracks in the edifice: in places like Lebanon and Uruguay, one can still have accounts in banks that are not registered as FATCA compliant. But by and large, the 30% withholding tax has acted as a powerful-enough deterrent. This episode teaches us a second important lesson: apparently, tax havens can be forced to cooperate if threatened with large-enough penalties.

Toward the Global Automatic Exchange of Information

The upshot of the American support in imposing FATCA is that it helped to strike a decisive blow against the flawed on-demand exchange policy. In 2013 the OECD recognized that the goal to be reached is an automatic exchange of data. The main high-income countries are now emulating the United States, and the automatic sharing of bank information is set to become the global standard by the end of this decade. Key havens—including Switzerland, Singapore, and Luxembourg—have already indicated that they would participate. In 2008 the vast majority of tax experts deemed such worldwide cooperation utopian. This huge step forward is a reason for optimism, and it teaches us a third lesson: new forms of cooperation, deemed impossible by many, can materialize in relatively short periods of time.

Despite all the progress made in curbing banking secrecy in recent years, we are still, in the spring of 2015, at the beginning—or almost—of the struggle against tax havens. The automatic exchange of bank information that is starting to be implemented comes up against three fundamental stumbling blocks.

First, outside of the United States, there has been no clear strategy presented to force tax havens to abandon financial secrecy. It is not enough to politely ask tax havens to cooperate. A number of them derive a large fraction of their income from illegal activities; if they have nothing to lose by continuing to attract tax dodgers, it is likely at least some will persist in this lucrative business. Yet no country, not even the European Union, has been able at this stage to articulate clear penalties like the United States has. Through diplomacy, the OECD has convinced many offshore centers to share bank information automatically. But the more havens that agree to cooperate, the bigger the incentives for the remaining ones not to do so. To believe that they will spontaneously give up managing the fortunes of the world's tax dodgers, without the threat of concrete sanctions, is to be guilty of extreme naïveté.

Even the penalties in FATCA in some ways do not go far enough. Banks who don't follow FATCA will suffer a 30% withholding tax on the interest and dividends they receive from the United States. Now, America might well be the largest economy on the planet, but defrauders can easily decide not to invest there. It is conceivable that in order to attract American clientele, some banks will voluntarily choose not to follow the FATCA law and invest, for themselves and for their clients, only in Europe or Asia. In those cases, they will incur no sanctions.

The second problem is that automatic information exchange is likely to come up against financial opacity. If you ask Swiss bankers if they have US, UK, or French clients, their response is always the same: "Very few," "fewer and fewer," and "soon, none at all." The overwhelming majority of accounts in tax havens are held through shell corporations, trusts, or foundations, all of which fulfill the same objective: to disconnect money from its true owners. The tricks (legal and illegal) that allow the wealthiest to claim they have abandoned control over their wealth—while conserving it in practice—are legion. What are the consequences of this? If ambitious measures are not taken to fight against this form of dissimulation, automatic information exchange may only involve a minority of taxpayers—those who do not have access to empty shells in which to hide their assets. All the while claiming that they are upholding their obligations, banks will be able to transmit only a relatively small fraction of their data to foreign countries every year—and may continue to protect the most aggressive defrauders.

Is this idle fancy? It is, however, this type of dissimulation that led the ancestor of FATCA—a US program called "qualified intermediary"—to fail. This program was in fact quite similar to the new law; at the time it was put into place at the beginning of the 2000s, many observers actually believed it would lead to the end of banking secrecy, since it already involved an automatic exchange of information. The main difference was that the banks were to provide the data only if their clients held American securities, whereas now they must cooperate regardless of the investments made by those clients. The fact remains that FATCA's predecessor was not enormously successful. Credit Suisse was thus one of the "qualified intermediaries" that was supposed to collaborate with the IRS. We know what happened, since in 2014 the Swiss bank pleaded guilty to criminal conspiracy to defraud the IRS and was sentenced to pay a fine of $2.6 billion for having actively solicited Americans and for having sold them services of tax evasion—notably by hiding their assets behind shell corporations. And Credit Suisse is far from being an isolated case: UBS, HSBC, and smaller establishments like Wegelin and BSI have been indicted by US authorities, have had to pay fines, or both; many others may have to in the near future.

The fundamental problem is that authorities have no means to verify that offshore bankers are respecting the spirit—or the letter—of international regulations. All the steps being taken today and the plans devised for the future are based on the idea that we can trust bankers to carry out their obligations. However, this belief is, to say the least, problematic. Many financiers in Switzerland and the Cayman Islands—a majority perhaps?—are honest people and will abide by the new law. But some may not. For decades, after all, bankers in Switzerland and elsewhere have been hiding their clients behind shell companies, smuggling diamonds in toothpaste tubes, handing bank statements concealed in sports magazine, all of this in violation of the law and the banks' stated policies. More than a handful rogue employees were involved: in 2008 over 1,800 Credit Suisse bankers were servicing Swiss accounts for US customers.[23] Some became enormously wealthy by doing so.

To ensure that bankers apply FATCA in practice, the American tax authorities rely on the denunciations of informers, to whom they promise fortunes. The IRS, for example, signed a check for $104 million to the ex-banker of the UBS, Bradley Birkenfeld, who revealed the practices of his former employer. But one may well doubt the effectiveness of this strategy. True, large organizations are today more than ever before at the mercy of information leaks, but whistle-blowing by rational (or moral) employees is less likely to occur in small firms than in big ones. If tax-evasion activities move to small boutique banks, shielded from US outreach, then enforcement might prove increasingly hard. To rely exclusively on whistle-blowers to fight against tax havens is not strong policy.

Even some large banks may straggle in a way that hinders enforcement, if they believe they are "too big to indict"—that is, they believe that regulators will hesitate to charge them because it might pose a danger to financial stability. In 2012 US authorities decided against indicting HSBC despite evidence that the bank enabled Mexican drug cartels to move money through its American subsidiaries, in violation of basic anti-money-laundering regulations. Instead, the bank was fined $1.92 billion, which pales in comparison to HSBC's pretax profits of $22.6 billion in 2013. And despite its guilty plea, Credit Suisse was able to keep its US banking license.

The final source of concern is that the largest international experiment in an automatic exchange of information most similar to FATCA, the EU savings tax directive, was a fiasco because it didn't include any measures for constraint, for fighting against opacity, or for verification. If we don't learn from all these lessons derived from experience, there is every reason to fear that the disaster will be repeated in the same way. This EU experiment therefore deserves a closer look.

The Lessons of the Savings Tax Directive

The savings tax directive was the star initiative of the European Union to fight against offshore tax evasion. By virtue of this directive, which has been applied since July 1, 2005, when a French resident, for example, earns interest on his English account, the United Kingdom automatically informs the French tax authority. In principle, this should make all fraud impossible. The savings tax directive could have been a great success, and in its time, it raised many hopes; but, in fact, it has been a great disappointment, due to three core mistakes.

First, although the directive is an EU-wide policy, not all European countries participate in it on an equal footing: Luxembourg and Austria were granted favorable terms. Those countries—the two EU tax havens for wealth management—do not have to automatically send information to the other member states (although this will hopefully change by 2018). This was the original sin: the exemptions accorded to Luxembourg and Austria have paralyzed the European struggle against tax havens for close to a decade. The EU had no credibility for imposing automatic exchanges on Switzerland and other non-European havens, since it is was not even capable of applying them to its own countries; in return, Luxembourg could give as justification the persistence of banking secrecy in Switzerland to block any revision of the savings tax directive. Seeing the large EU countries capitulate before such obvious maneuvering for years and years is the tragedy of the European construction.

Instead of an exchange of information, Luxembourg and Austria apply a withholding tax: Luxembourg banks must tax at 35% the interest earned by French residents on their accounts there. Three-quarters of this tax is then sent to France. Thirty-five percent is less than the top marginal income tax rate in force in France: oddly enough, the holders of hidden accounts thus find themselves having the "right" to pay less tax than honest taxpayers. An identical tax is applied in most of the tax havens outside the European Union—with the exception of Singapore and Hong Kong, but including Switzerland—who have signed agreements with the EU to have the same rules as Austria and Luxembourg applied.

The fixed tax (35% regardless of the income or the wealth of the taxpayer) makes little sense. There is no reason to tax at the same rate income from a million Euros and that from a few hundred. And it violates the fiscal sovereignty of EU countries that can no longer choose the rate at which they wish to tax the interest of their residents. Tax havens, primarily Luxembourg, are the first to defend the right of each country to choose its tax rate; they are also the first to flout this principle on a daily basis.

The second defect of the EU savings tax directive is the most serious: the concession of a fixed tax of 35% doesn't even work. The directive in fact applies only to accounts held in the name of the owners, not to those held through the intermediary of shell corporations, trusts, or foundations. The Swiss tax administration explained this candidly to Swiss banks, in a memo regarding the agreement passed with the EU for the application of the directive on its territory: "Interest payments to legal entities do not fall within the scope of the agreement" (paragraph 29).[24] But what is a "legal entity"? The response is in paragraph 31, which provides a "partial" inventory of them: companies in the Cayman Islands, those of the Virgin Islands, trusts and companies in the Bahamas, companies and foundations in Panama, trusts, holdings, and foundations in Liechtenstein, and so on.

At least this is clear! Owners of Swiss or Luxembourg accounts have only to transfer their assets to any shell structure to escape the fixed tax of 35%. Creating shell companies costs a few hundred dollars and is done in just a few minutes.

But there is a final loophole. The directive only applies to interest income, not to dividends. Why? This is a mystery. There is no valid economic reason to treat these two categories of income differently. As we have seen, wealthy households do not turn to tax havens to let their money sleep in accounts that earn little interest. Close to two-thirds of their assets are invested in stocks and shares of mutual funds that pay dividends. In other words, from the onset, the directive arbitrarily excludes most dissimulated wealth from its realm of influence. Fortunately, FATCA and similar laws that will enter into force by the end of this decade are much broader in scope: they include all types of capital-income payments, including dividends, capital gains, and insurance payments. One should not, however, underestimate the ingenuity of bankers when it comes to dodging regulations: using derivatives, some might be well able to generate income falling outside the scope of FATCA. Only time will tell.

Fifteen years of negotiations in Europe—the first discussions began at the beginning of the 1990s—to end with this: a directive filled with holes that shows absolutely no serious will to fight against financial dissimulation. Was it from lethargy that the European authorities agreed to exclude shell corporations from the perimeter of the savings tax directive? Was it incompetence? Complicity? We don't know. The sociology of this embarrassing episode remains to be written. In the meantime, we can at least investigate its economic effects.

Not surprisingly, the main effect of the savings tax directive has been to encourage Europeans who hadn't already done so to transfer their wealth to shell corporations, trusts, and foundations. This occurred on a massive scale in Switzerland, the country for which we have the best statistics (see fig. 5). At the end of 2004, right before the directive was put into effect, 50% of the accounts in Switzerland already "belonged" on paper to shell companies and 25% to Europeans in their own names. At the end of 2005, six months after the introduction of the 35% withholding tax, Europeans "possessed" only 15% of the accounts (–10%), and shell corporations 60% (+10%). It only took a few mouse clicks, a few pieces of paper printed in Geneva and Zurich, to transfer the ownership of tens of billions

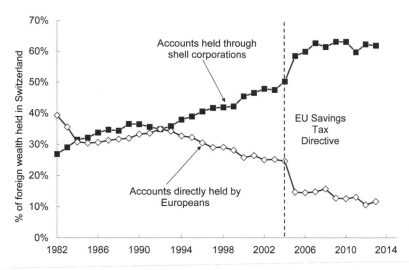

Figure 5: Who holds accounts in Switzerland? The effect of the 2005 savings tax directive.

Source: BNS (see online appendix to chapter 3, www.gabriel-zucman.eu).

of dollars to trusts in the Virgin Islands or to Liechtenstein foundations. The creation of these structures takes place right in Switzerland, in the banks, trusts, and wealth-management offices. Nothing happens in the Virgin Islands. Swiss bankers have deliberately, and on a large scale, torpedoed the savings tax directive.

If all the interest and dividends earned in Switzerland by residents of the European Union were indeed subject to a tax of 35%, this tax would earn on the order of €20 billion per year. In 2012 Switzerland paid €300 million to the EU, about sixty times less. This theft goes on and on, year after year, apparently without really troubling either Swiss bankers, who today depict themselves as paragons of virtue, or European politicians, who like to congratulate themselves on their great determination in fighting tax evasion.

The lack of sanctions for nonparticipating havens, dissimulation through shell corporations, and the blind faith in bankers made the directive fail. Without heeding the lessons from this episode, there is a real chance that they will do the same with the FATCA and similar laws. Most tax havens have promised to proceed to automatic information exchanges in 2017–18, but as the former prime minister of Luxembourg (now president of the European Commission) Jean-Claude Juncker candidly admitted: "The lights are not going to go out in banks" of offshore centers like the Grand Duchy for all that; defrauders may remain protected by their trusts and other empty shells.[25] Sanctions are not mentioned anywhere nor is verification. How can we think today—in light of what happened in 2005 and the UBS and Credit Suisse cases in the United States—that Swiss bankers will cooperate of their own free will, in good faith? It is high time we wake up to reality.

FOUR

What to Do?
A New Approach

To fight offshore tax evasion effectively, we need a set of coherent and focused measures: concrete sanctions proportional to the costs imposed by uncooperative tax havens to other countries and an international financial register.

Financial and Commercial Sanctions

First, there must be constraints. The tax havens that assist defrauders themselves derive substantial, sometimes huge profit from their activities. In some microstates, most of government revenue derives from fees levied on the incorporation of shell companies, trusts, and similar arrangements. Thanks to financial secrecy, others manage to attract real activity—such as bank offices, audit firms, and law firms—generating employment, profits, and taxes at the expense of their neighbors. For the most successful havens, the profits are political. Luxembourg is a case in point: the outsize role played by the tiny Grand Duchy in world financial markets has directly benefited its political elite for decades, enabling some of its members to occupy key positions in European institutions. If they have nothing to lose by continuing to attract tax dodgers, it is likely at least some tax havens and their elite will continue this lucrative business. Concrete threats, on the other hand, have the potential to make them bend.

An illustration of this is the blockade that France imposed on Monaco in 1962. At that time, French citizens who were living in the principality paid no tax on their income. The French government wanted to put an end to this situation, but Prince Rainier was firm: there would be no question of challenging the fiscal sovereignty of Monaco. France could have stopped there and, after endless summit discussions, given in to the demands of the microstate—as the large countries of Europe have done for years with Luxembourg. But de Gaulle would not budge. On the night of October 12–13, 1962, he sent customs officers to rebuild the border between France and Monaco. The message was clear: if it didn't cooperate, Monaco would be cut off from the world. And the results were immediate—since 1963 French people who live in Monaco are subject to the same fiscal laws as those who live in France proper.

There are several important differences between the current situation and that of 1962, but what is clear is that the ratio of strength is eminently in favor of the large countries, not of the microstates that have specialized in services of financial opacity and in helping defrauders.

In concrete terms, how can they be induced to cooperate? A simple solution consists of following and expanding the US approach with FATCA—that is, taxing the interest and dividends paid to those countries, in an effort coordinated between the United States, Europe, and other G20 economies. Some countries have already been imposing taxes similar to those introduced by the recent American legislation, but they are very limited in scope. For example, France currently imposes a tax of 50% on the income that leaves the country in the direction of what it considers to be "noncooperative territories," meaning Botswana, Brunei, Guatemala, the Marshall Islands, Montserrat, Nauru, the Island of Niue, and the British Virgin Islands. Unfortunately, lists of noncooperative territories (the OECD, the IMF, and the G20 all have had one at some point) always end up including only a number of small, unpopulated havens—like in the French case—disregarding the places where the bulk of tax fraud takes place. It is high time for G20 countries to emulate the US approach and impose systematic penalties for noncompliance.

As the recent work of the OECD on automatic information exchange shows, sanctions are not always necessary: diplomacy can go a long way in securing formal commitments. But not all tax havens are on board; and in the absence of well-defined penalties, history suggests that formal commitments may not translate into real change: threats may be necessary to foster effective cooperation.

Although financial sanctions are appealing and simple to implement, they face a potential obstacle: they can be easily circumvented. A bank that does not want to comply with FATCA could use FATCA-compliant intermediaries to continue investing in the United States without facing the 30% US withholding tax. The US law contains provisions to prevent this scenario, but the opacity of financial intermediation chains (largely because of the absence of financial registers) is such that these provisions may well not be enough.

An alternative approach to withholding taxes consists of acting on the level of the trade of goods and services, which are currently more traceable than financial transactions. Tax havens cannot, in fact, do without commercial avenues. For the United States and Japan, exports represent a total of only 15% of their GDP. But they weigh in at 50% of Switzerland's GDP and up to 200% in Luxembourg, Singapore, and Hong Kong, the three countries that hold the world record in exports. Granted, these spectacular percentages are artificially inflated by companies' practices of fiscal optimization, as well as by entrepôt trade in countries such as Hong Kong, a territory through which flows a large part of the imports and exports from China. In spite of all this, the percentages also correspond to a basic reality: the crucial nature of international trade in the economies of small countries. In a small, introverted economy, producers have access only to a restricted market and cannot easily specialize. Only access to world commerce enables them to achieve an increase in profits, to increase a division of labor, and, ultimately, to achieve levels of productivity found in large countries. Without access to foreign markets, tax havens are condemned to die.

Justified and Realistic Sanctions

Imposing trade tariffs on uncooperative tax havens is well-founded in economic reasoning. Each year financial secrecy—

the lack of effective exchange of information between offshore banks and foreign authorities—deprives governments around the world of about $200 billion. It's important to understand that we're not talking about tax competition, but of theft pure and simple: Switzerland, Luxembourg, or the Cayman Islands offer some taxpayers who wish to do so the possibility of stealing from their governments. It is their choice, but there is no reason that the United States, Europe, or developing countries should pay the price for it. Financial secrecy—like greenhouse gas emissions—has a costly impact on the entire world, which tax havens choose to ignore. In economic lingo, it is a matter of negative externality. The solution to this problem was proposed in the work of the English economist Arthur Pigou a century ago: it is a tax equal to the losses incurred by foreign countries.

In other terms, zero or limited cooperation is a disguised form of subvention. It gives offshore financial institutions a competitive advantage, just as the absence of environmental protections allows polluting companies to be more competitive. Now, these forms of hidden subvention inhibit the good functioning of markets. This is precisely one of the missions of the World Trade Organization, to discourage disloyal practices of this type, by authorizing countries who are victims of it to impose supplemental customs duties to compensate for the losses they incur.

The problem with this type of approach is that it is difficult to quantify the exact cost of anti-competitive practices. That is why it is important to measure hidden wealth and the loss in tax revenue that it creates. The estimates that this book proposes provide a start, because they are based on official statistics and verifiable calculations. The tax havens that feel wronged are free to produce their own estimates—under the condition, of course, that they are consistent with the available data, in particular with the gaping statistical anomalies in the portfolio positions of countries.

Trade tariffs are also realistic because, even though the main offshore centers are financial giants, they are not great commercial powers. Granted, there are two risks in this approach. First, that of escalation: Switzerland might react to French tariffs, for example, by increasing its own customs duties or by closing its borders to tourists or cross-border workers. No one would gain from such a commercial war. But there is a way to avoid this: create a coalition of countries strong enough so that Bern would have no interest in playing that game. It is conceivable that Switzerland might want to retaliate against France, but certainly not against the main European powers combined, because that would certainly mean its ruin.[26]

The second risk is that commercial sanctions might not be enough. Hong Kong, for example, might prefer to endure French tariffs—even prohibitive ones—rather than abandon its financial secrecy. The solution, again, is to create an international coalition that includes countries that weigh heavily in Hong Kong's foreign trade.

This, then, is the essential difference with the Monaco episode of 1962: alone, countries like France cannot achieve very much. Only combined international pressure can truly have an impact. The solution exists nevertheless: coalitions of countries can make the principal tax havens bend by imposing trade tariffs equal to the cost of financial secrecy.

A Plan for Customs Tariffs

Concretely, what do winning coalitions look like? There is a trade-off: small coalitions are easier to form, but there is a higher risk that tax havens will play the escalation game. By contrast, in a large coalition the risk of commercial war is small, but alliances of this type are more difficult to form. In practice, exports from the main offshore centers are quite concentrated on a limited number of partners, so that it would be enough for a handful of countries to join together for uncooperative territories to endure very high losses, without, however, daring to launch retaliations. The optimal coalitions are thus small and therefore easy to form.

Let's take the example of Switzerland—the argument applies similarly to Dubai, Macau, or any other country that might be tempted to do in the twenty-first century what Switzerland pioneered in the twentieth, namely, helping defrauders evade their home countries' laws. Germany, France, and Italy represent about 35% of Switzerland's exports, but for them Switzerland is only a small client (scarcely 5% of their exports): any commercial war would mathematically end up with the defeat of Bern. Thus this would be a coalition against which Switzerland would have no interest in putting up resistance.

What customs duties should be imposed? By definition, the only justifiable tariff from the point of view of the WTO is the one that enables the recovery of the costs of financial secrecy. Following this logic, and according to my calculations, Germany, France, and Italy have the right to impose a tariff of 30% on the goods they import from Switzerland. As we saw in chapter 1, these three countries have a total of around €500 billion in Swiss banks, of which about 80% still evades taxes today. This represents a loss of fiscal revenue of around €15 billion (tax on income, on inheritance, and, in the case of France, wealth tax). And €15 billion is the sum it is possible to recover with a tariff of 30% on goods coming from Switzerland.

There are two remarks to be made on these figures. First, the loss of revenue due to financial secrecy is estimated *a minima*, because it doesn't include the cost of tax reductions that governments have had to agree to for fear that their taxpayers will hide their wealth in Switzerland. Now, these costs are significant, especially in Italy, the country that has gone the farthest in lowering taxes on financial capital. Dividends there today are taxed at only 20% (much lower than labor income), inheritances are almost exonerated, and the belief that it is impossible to tax financial wealth is so widespread that only real estate holdings have been affected by the latest tax increase—a policy that, moreover, led to the defeat of Mario Monti in the 2013 elections. Let's prefer cautious calculations of loss, however, because then there can be no reason for them to be contested before the WTO.

A second remark: in any calculation of optimal customs duties, there is a margin of error, because we never know what exactly will be the reaction of exporters and importers, as it depends on many parameters. But a likely scenario might look like this: should a tariff be imposed, French customers would stop purchasing Swiss products unless the after-tax prices of these products remain unchanged, those prices being determined on a global level. So Swiss producers would have to sell less and cut their pretax price: instead of exporting, as they currently do, €60 billion worth of goods to France, Germany, and Italy—primarily chemical products, machines, and watches—they would sell no more than €45 billion worth, which, after paying the tariff of 30%, would correspond to an unchanged invoice of around €60 billion for the importers. And so there would be a decrease of €15 billion in national income for Switzerland and a corresponding increase for the three border countries.

In all likelihood, a loss of €15 billion would be enough to force Switzerland to cooperate truthfully, because it is a sum comparable to what it earns in total by managing the wealth of tax evaders. According to official statistics, the financial sector represents around 11% of Switzerland's GDP. But private wealth-management activities strictly speaking account for only 4%. The rest corresponds to the activity of insurers and other banking businesses, loans, proprietary trading, and so on. Furthermore, the wealth managed by Swiss banks is not all hidden—that of the Swiss is for the most part indeed declared—so that tax evasion scarcely brings in more than 3% of the GDP (around 1% of the total amount of undeclared assets managed by the banks), or €15 billion per year. This is an appreciable, but not vital, contribution: contrary to a common notion, Switzerland does not live off of financial opacity (unlike some microstates), and it would do very well if it completely disappeared.

There is, of course, uncertainty about what exactly Switzerland earns, and 3% of the GDP is conservative, in particular because the wealth of defrauders involves activity in places other than in banks' departments of wealth management. But the important point is that tax evasion earns Switzerland much less than what it costs the countries that are victims of it. If Swiss banks were the only ones in the world to provide services of tax evasion, they could in principle raise their commissions and earn the equivalent of all, or almost all, of the tax evaded by their clients. But they are no longer a monopoly and cannot charge the exorbitant commissions they did in the 1960s.

If the customs duties of 30% proved ineffective (for example, due to the political influence of Swiss bankers), it would be enough to enlarge the coalition to other countries: by including the United Kingdom, Spain, and Belgium, losses for Switzerland would reach 4% of the GDP; with the entire European Union, 5%. The more governments in the coalition, the greater are the chances for success. But the good news is that all it would take is a small group (France, Germany, and Italy, or the United Kingdom) to force the full cooperation of Swiss banks and authorities.

This must be stated clearly: the goal of commercial sanctions is to force tax havens to cooperate, not to establish protectionism. We're talking about threats to agitate, which ideally will never have to be applied. Customs duties of 30% have never lastingly profited anyone. In the long term, free exchange benefits all nations and protectionism is to be avoided. But quite simply, we can no longer continue to liberalize trade while completely ignoring the problems of fiscal dissimulation.

Those problems must be placed at the heart of discussions on trade. Since tariffs/sanctions are realistic and proportional, they are credible and, therefore, in principle they will not need to be applied. But if discussions aren't enough, they should be put into effect.

In any event, there is no progress possible without specific threats. The great majority of Swiss citizens and Swiss companies have nothing to lose with full financial transparency and would certainly prefer that offshore tax evasion disappears rather than see their country regularly singled out. But bankers have a political influence that far exceeds their true economic weight, so that, without threats of reprisals, there is good reason to fear that they will succeed in maintaining a form of status quo—for instance, abandoning a portion of their clientele, those who do not have the means to hide assets in trusts, while at the same time concentrating on the greatest wealth.

The same approach would lead to the cooperation of other large centers. In all cases, the large countries can legally make the giants of offshore banking bend, using relatively small coalitions.

The Case of Luxembourg

One country poses a problem, however, because it is protected from trade tariffs through European treaties: Luxembourg. Should it be excluded from the EU? The question deserves to be asked, because the Luxembourg that cofounded the Union in 1957 has nothing to do with the Luxembourg of today. Steel was everything back then; finance was nothing. Today, without

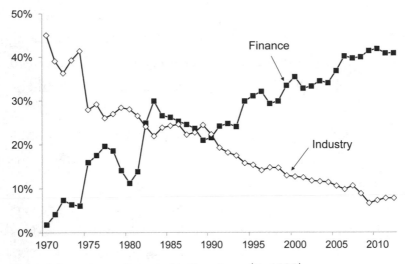

Figure 6: Luxembourg: From steel to Clearstream (% of GDP).
Source: Statec (see online appendix to chapter 4, www.gabriel-zucman.eu).

its financial industry, the Grand Duchy would be nothing; tomorrow, offshore finance may be everything (see fig. 6). It is the tax haven of all tax havens, present in all stages of the circuit of international wealth management, used by all other financial centers.

The signatories of the Treaty of Rome could not have envisioned the possibility of such an upheaval when they established the bases of European institutions. For them, Luxembourg was an old nation, the heir of a member state of the Germanic Holy Roman Empire since 1000, which had been a resolute proponent of the European dream. Today the trap has shut. An economic colony of the international financial industry, Luxembourg is at the heart of European tax evasion and has paralyzed the struggle against this scourge for decades.

This great transformation deserves to be recounted, if we

wish to find a rational way to remedy it. First, it is important to understand that Luxembourg does not owe the success of its conversion to its so-called stability or its highly qualified labor force, as its proponents claim. In reality, inflation there has been almost as high as in France since the 1970s and much higher than in Germany. Economic activity fluctuates violently depending on the jolts of international finance: between 2007 and 2009, the GDP per worker was lowered by 10% (as opposed to 2% in France); it has not gone up much since. The only stability is that of power: since 1783 the reigning family, the Nassaus, has transferred from one branch of the family to another the title of grand duke; the Christian Social People's Party has provided the prime minister since the end of the Second World War, with the exception of a short period of five years at the end of the 1970s and of the government elected in 2013. As for the national labor force, it is aging and has nothing unique to sell: not steel, not ancestral tradition for wealth management as in Switzerland, nor prestigious university diplomas as in Great Britain.

If Luxembourg has succeeded in becoming one of the foremost financial centers in the world, it has been by commercializing its own sovereignty.[27] Starting in the 1970s, the government initiated an unheard-of enterprise: the sale to multinationals throughout the world of the right to decide their own rate of taxation, regulatory constraints, and legal obligations for themselves. There were many who saw the advantage of this new type of trade. Does a large bank want to create an investment fund for its clients? Let it set it up in the Grand Duchy; the government imposes no taxes. Does the same bank wish to sell new stocks to strengthen its capital and satisfy the demands of regulators? In Luxembourg it can issue "hybrid" securities: stocks for the supervisors but bonds for the tax authority—the income paid will be deductible from the corporate income tax. In the fall of 2014, a consortium of investigative journalists revealed a large number of discretionary deals signed by the Luxembourg tax authority with multinational companies from all over the world, granting them low or zero effective tax rates on their profits.

The trade of sovereignty knows no limits. Everything is bought; everything is negotiable. It has attracted thousands of investment funds, the holdings of multinational groups, shell companies, and private banks. The installation of companies, in turn, has brought workers in finance, auditing, and consulting. There are currently more than 150,000 people who cross the border twice every day, half from France, a quarter each from Belgium and Germany.

Luxembourg is not the only country that has sold its sovereignty, far from it. Many microstates have given in to the temptation. But it is the one that has gone the furthest. In 2013 one-third of the production of the Grand Duchy was used to pay the salaries of cross-border workers and, above all, the income owed to the foreign owners of banks, investment funds, and holdings. The GNP thus represents only two-thirds of the GDP: after the deduction of the net primary income paid to the rest of the world—salaries, dividends, and interest—the GDP of Luxembourg is reduced by a third.

This situation is unique in the world and in history: no independent nation, no matter how small and open to international trade, has ever paid such a share of its income abroad. A single territory today comes close to rivaling the Grand Duchy in this regard: Puerto Rico. The archipelago of the Caribbean, with close to 4 million inhabitants, is a tax haven sought after by multinationals, notably drug companies. All, or almost all, of the capital there is held by Americans, who hire the local population; all profits return to Uncle Sam. The difference with Luxembourg is that Puerto Rico is not an independent nation. The US Congress imposes most of the laws there, but the local population does not have American citizenship. It cannot elect a senator, a representative, or the president of the United States.

Imagine an ocean platform where the inhabitants would meet during the day to produce and trade, free of any law or any tax, before being teleported in the evening back home to their families on the mainland. No one would dream of considering such a place, where 100% of its production is sent abroad, as a nation. What is a nation, what is a platform? We don't know where to set the limit, but a threshold of 50% of its production, which Luxembourg is approaching and which it could reach by 2020, is not unreasonable.

Is Luxembourg In or Out?

Let's be clear: if Luxembourg is no longer a nation, it no longer has a place in the European Union. At the Council of the European Union (which gathers together the ministers of the member states) and the European Council (where the heads of state and government determine strategic goals), each country, however small, can make its voice heard. But nothing in the treaties, in the spirit of European construction or in democratic reasoning, justifies allowing an offshore platform for the global financial industry to have a voice equal to that of other countries. And this especially since the Grand Duchy, like every member state, has extensive blocking capabilities. In the Council of the European Union, each country has a right to veto proposals related to taxation, social policy, and foreign affairs. In the European Council, decisions are made unanimously. In both these institutions where most power is exercised, the representative of the 500,000 inhabitants of Luxembourg can impose his will on 500 million Europeans. Will we ever discover all the obstructions and compromises imposed by him? Undoubtedly not, because the deliberations of the European Council (and certain meetings of finance ministers) are held in secret, about which the prime minister from Luxembourg publicly congratulated himself, by the way.

The other problem raised by Luxembourg in its current form belonging to the EU is the threat that it represents to the financial stability of the Union. Because the economic model of the Grand Duchy is based on a hypertrophic financial sector, it is not viable and risks ending in catastrophe, as happened in Ireland or Cyprus, with a costly bailout as a result. It is also a model that, contrary to popular belief, has not benefited the local population. The GDP per worker has grown by only 1.4% per year since 1970, a very mediocre result that places Luxembourg at the back of the line of developed countries.

Inequality among the inhabitants, on the other hand, has taken off. Salaries in the offshore sector have exploded, in particular in judicial and business consulting activities. In the manufacturing industry, construction, or transportation, workers have not benefited from any gain in purchasing power for twenty years and have seen their relative position collapse. Since 1980 the poverty rate has doubled; housing prices have tripled. Luxembourg City—with 100,000 inhabitants, granted, green, and fortified, but of frankly limited attraction—is today as expensive as London. The country is cut in two: bankers, lawyers, and accountants live in opulence, while the rest of the population suffers an accelerated decline. And those excluded from the world of finance should not count very much on school: educational performance, according to PISA (Programme for International Student Assessment) surveys, is among the worst of the countries of the OECD and scholastic inequalities among the highest.

If we wish to prevent the Irish and Cypriot catastrophes from happening again, it is essential that Luxembourg go backward. The simplest solution is full and complete cooperation with foreign countries to stop fraud and put an end to the fiscal optimization of large companies. This operation of transparency will cost the Grand Duchy a lot (at least 30% of the GDP), because the financial sector in Luxembourg literally lives off of the accounting manipulation of multinationals and the fraud of individuals, not only from financial secrecy, which brings in close to 10% of the GDP, but above all because a large portion of the money held in Switzerland and elsewhere is recycled through its investment funds. Unless Luxembourg cooperates, the threat to be made is clear: exclusion from the EU, followed by a financial and trade embargo by the three bordering countries.

A Global Financial Register

Now that we have analyzed the first element in a plan of action—sanctions against uncooperative territories—let's look at the second, the creation of tools for verification. When tax havens agree to cooperate, how can we ensure that they do so in practice?

The primary objective, and one of the central propositions formulated in this book, is to create a global financial register. Quite simply, it would be a register recording who owns all the financial securities in circulation, stocks, bonds, and shares of mutual funds throughout the world. A register of this type is useful because it would enable tax authorities to check that banks, onshore and above all offshore, are in fact transmitting all of the data they have available. Without a register of this type, Swiss bankers will always be able to claim that they don't have any US or UK clients and can continue to communicate very little information to the IRS or HMRC. That is what history teaches us: from the large-scale falsification of bank documents by Swiss establishments in 1945, to the fiasco of the savings tax directive and of the "qualified intermediary" program in the United States, everything points to the need for verification tools that do not exclusively rely on the good-will of offshore bankers. Without concrete ways to verify that bankers duly transmit the information they have about their customers, wealthy tax dodgers may be able to hide in all impunity an ever-rising portion of their wealth.

But the goal of the register extends beyond curbing tax evasion: a better accounting of wealth—not only real assets but also financial claims—would do much good in the fight against money laundering, bribery, and the financing of terrorism, and it would help better monitor financial stability. A financial register is a concrete embodiment of the notion of financial transparency.

A global financial register is in no way utopian, because similar registers already exist—but they are scattered and under the management of private companies. The goal is to combine them in order to create a global register that is used for the public good.

To understand the functioning of this register, its usefulness and feasibility, it is first necessary to know what the partial registers that exist today actually do. As we have seen in chapter 1, stocks and bonds were in the form of pieces of paper during the greater part of the twentieth century. One had to move securities from bank to bank with each transaction, which was particularly laborious. With growth in the postwar period, the amount of securities became considerable, and the system was on the edge of asphyxia. To remedy this situation, in the 1960s (sometimes a bit earlier) every country created a central depository where the securities were kept. In the United States, for example, it is the Depository Trust Company, founded in 1973, that nowadays keeps all the securities issued by American companies in its safes (the Federal

Bank of New York does the same for government bonds). Each bank has an account with the DTC; when one of their clients sells a security, their account is debited and that of the bank of the buyer is credited. Pieces of paper are no longer circulated. Once immobilized in the 1960s, securities quickly were dematerialized: the paper disappeared entirely, and the DTC simply records on its computers the data of who holds what.

Every country does the same and has its own central depository. But this system has a defect. Since the 1960s American companies have had the habit of issuing bonds in marks or in pounds sterling, directly outside the US territory, on the German or English markets. These stateless securities, not really American not really European, have no natural central depository. Two companies filled this void and play the role of register for them: Euroclear in Belgium and Cedel in Luxembourg, today known by the name of Clearstream.

The importance of the activity of this latter company and the myths that surround it beg a quick clarification. First, the name of Clearstream is a misnomer. The original—and still primary—activity of this company is that of central depository, meaning it keeps stateless bonds (once in paper form, today electronic) at a secure site and maintains a register of the owners. This is stock management. It was only recently that Clearstream began to play the role of clearinghouse, an activity that manages the flow of transactions. This consists of establishing, at the end of each day, the commitments that all buyers and sellers on the market have with one another, in order to transform the millions of gross orders into a limited number of net operations. This clearinghouse activity is of marginal interest in the struggle against tax havens, unlike that of a central depository, because Clearstream and Euroclear are today the only two entities capable of authenticating the owners of trillions of dollars of stateless securities.

To create a world financial register, the first step would involve merging the computer data of the DTC (for American securities), Euroclear Belgium and Clearstream (for stateless securities), Euroclear France (for French securities), and of all the other national central depositories. Who should be in charge of this mission? Ideally, global public goods are best provided by international institutions. One candidate is the International Monetary Fund, one of the only international organizations that is truly global—all countries are members of it, with very rare exceptions. The IMF has the technical capabilities to create a register and to have it function in the medium term; it is also the institution that establishes international statistical rules and is responsible for collecting data on the flow of capital and countries' portfolio positions, which, as we have seen, currently suffer serious anomalies (in particular a gaping disequilibrium between assets and liabilities). A register would precisely enable the resolution of these problems, which seriously handicap the surveillance of financial stability. In the short run, a realistic plan of action probably involves the creation of partial registers at the regional level (say, a European register managed by the European Central Bank) and the progressive merging of the regional registers to ultimately cover all of the world's stocks and bonds.

A key challenge faced by any register of wealth involves the identification of beneficial owners. All of the world's wealth ultimately belongs to real people, with the exception of government-owned assets and the wealth of most nonprofit institutions, like university endowments. But a large fraction of the world's securities might not initially be attributable to any well-identified person: equities and bonds are largely held through intertwined financial intermediaries, like mutual funds, pension funds, and the like. Most depositories do not record the names of the real owners in their files, only those of intermediaries through which securities are transferred. To identify the residence of the ultimate owner, it would be necessary to know the relationships of the different entities involved in the wealth-holding chain. Fortunately, progress has begun in this area since the 2008–9 financial crisis, under the auspices of a committee of authorities from around the world working to create a global system of legal entity identification.[28] Furthermore, by virtue of the international anti-laundering regulations, authorities have the right to demand that the depositories correctly identify the true holders of securities, by going back up the chain of financial intermediation if necessary. This is the fundamental principle in the fight against money laundering and the financing of terrorism: all establishments should know the names and addresses of their actual clients.

One concern that some readers will probably have is that a world financial register would threaten individual privacy. Yet countries have property records for land and real estate; these records are public, and there seems to be little misuse. Anybody, for example, can check online who owns real estate on Park Avenue (although one sometimes stumbles upon

faceless corporate titles) or if a particular person owns anything in Brooklyn. Of course, these records about real estate
only capture part of people's wealth, but when the records
were created, centuries ago, land accounted for the bulk of
private wealth, so that they indeed recorded most of people's
fortunes. The notion that a register of financial wealth would
be a radical departure from earlier practices concerning privacy is wrong, and in light of historical experience, it would
be natural to make the world financial register public just like
real estate records are.

However, it is also true that not all countries have the
same attitudes toward transparency, and such attitudes change
over time. In some Scandinavian countries, taxpayers' income
and wealth is made public. But not in the United States today, although income tax payments there were required to
be publicly disclosed in 1923 and 1924. So there might be a
case for keeping the world financial register confidentially in
the hands of the authorities. Whatever public body manages
the register, access to it should be granted to domestic fiscal
administrations, in order to enable them to verify that all the
securities held by their taxpayers are indeed declared—and
in particular that the offshore banks are exchanging all the
information they have (see fig. 7).

In the short term, the world financial register would not
include all financial wealth, only stocks, bonds, and shares
in investment funds. There is currently no complete private
register for derivative products—the few registers created in
the aftermath of the financial crisis are still partial. This is an
important gap, which seriously handicaps the oversight of

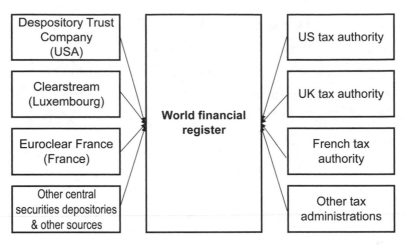

Figure 7: The case for a global financial register. The companies Clearstream, Euroclear, and so on feed the world financial register. Tax authorities can verify that taxpayers indeed declare all the financial securities included in the register. *Source:* Depository Trust Company (USA).

financial stability and which, if it is not filled in, could ultimately ruin the plan I propose—because tax dodgers could then convert all their securities into options, warrants, and so on. This is why it is essential that the global register, once it is created from the exhaustive registers that exist for securities, be extended to include derivatives as quickly as possible. More than a simple question of fiscal importance, it is a critical element for the regulation of financial markets.

A Tax on Capital

The world financial register is intimately linked to the proposal for a global wealth tax made by Thomas Piketty in *Capital in the Twenty-First Century.* This proposal has generated a heated controversy, and I don't want to repeat it here. Quite simply, let's assume that a tax on wealth might turn out to be desirable in certain places, at certain times, if wealth concentration was to reach extreme levels above which inequality harms growth, innovation, or the well functioning of our democratic institutions. How would the wealth tax work? It is not possible to tax wealth if we cannot measure it. Most people are honest and would pay the tax if it existed, but if even a tiny minority of tax dodgers could freely evade it, the consent to taxation would be severely undermined. On the contrary, the financial register that I describe, combined with the land and real estate registers that are already in place, would make it possible to enforce wealth taxes in a democratic and transparent way. The register is thus a necessary tool for the taxation of wealth in the twenty-first century.

It is actually the combination of wealth taxation and financial registries that would deal the fatal blow to financial opacity. Without a wealth tax, there is a risk that even a global register might fail to identify who exactly owns what. Despite anti-laundering legislation that requires financial institutions to know who the owners of the wealth that they have in their accounts truly are, a not negligible portion of the securities could continue to be recorded in a register as belonging to trusts without a well-identified owner. We can even imagine that a large-scale trade in identities might develop, in which individuals would claim to hold the wealth of defrauders or drug traffickers. A small tax on wealth levied at the source, however, would address this problem.

Let's look at a concrete case: imagine a global tax of 0.1% on the stock of wealth withheld at the source. This means that each year tax authorities, drawing on the information in the register, would deduct 0.1% of the value of all financial securities, bank accounts, and so on. In order to recover what has been taken from them, US taxpayers, for example, would have only one solution: declare their holdings on their IRS tax returns. Subject to this declaration, they would receive a credit for any taxes that remain due—or see themselves reimbursed if they owe no taxes at all.

This solution has four advantages. First, it is realistic: taxing 0.1% at the source is not utopian. An identical tax already exists in several countries, such as Switzerland, where all companies must, before paying any interest or dividend whatsoever, withhold a reimbursable tax of 35%. The difference with the tax that I propose is that mine is global—all financial securities would be subject, and not, as in Switzerland, only Swiss securities—and imposed as a percentage of wealth (0.1% of the value of the stock of assets) rather than income (35% of the interest and dividends generated by stocks and bonds), because many securities do not generate any income. With the establishment of a global register, these two differences pose no practical problem. There would be no escaping taxation.

The second advantage is that each country would preserve its fiscal sovereignty, because the tax would be reimbursable to the owners of securities once they have declared them in their country. States that do not wish to tax wealth would return all of the tax levied for them. The countries who wish to impose a progressive rate would be free to continue to do so.

The third and primary advantage: a global tax at the source would greatly reduce the use of shell corporations, trusts, foundations, names-only, and all imaginable techniques for dissimulation. For a simple reason: it would be reimbursable only after the wealth is declared on individual tax returns. Those who wish to hide their wealth would have no other choice than to pay the tax. Taxation on capital at the source is the ultimate weapon against financial opacity (although, in order to dissuade anyone from hiding wealth, one would need a wealth tax at a sufficiently elevated rate, more than 0.1% a year).

Finally, a coordinated global tax at the source, combined with the financial register described above, would give states that want it the possibility of creating their own tax on wealth, with a wide base and at a progressive rate, without having to fear evasion. In many countries, it is precisely such fears that in the last few years have led to the elimination of the existing taxes on wealth. But this doesn't have to be the case: nations can recover the sovereignty that has been stolen from them, and they can act against the rise of inequality if they wish.

FIVE

The Tax Avoidance of Multinational Corporations

Offshore tax havens enable not only individuals to dodge taxes—they also enable multinational corporations to do so. Often this tax avoidance is done within the letter of the law: multinational groups exploit the loopholes of current legislation. The fundamental problem is that the corporate tax is not adapted anymore to today's globalized world and must be reinvented. The spiral is profound, but here, too, solutions exist.[29]

From Mountain View to Bermuda

The reason for the current failure is that the corporate tax is based on a fiction, the idea that one can establish the profits earned by each multinational subsidiary by subsidiary. But this fiction is no longer tenable today, because multinational groups, advised by great auditing and consulting firms, are in practice free to move their profits wherever they want, which is usually wherever it is taxed the least; and large countries have themselves mostly given up taxing the profits booked outside of their territory.

How do companies make their profits appear in tax havens? There are two main techniques. The first, that of intragroup loans, consists of loading with debt branches located in countries that tax profits heavily, such as France and the United States. The goal is to reduce the profits where they are taxed and have them appear in Luxembourg or in Bermuda, where they are taxed very little or not at all. This popular manipulation nevertheless comes up against a sizable problem: it is rather easy to detect.

The second optimization technique, the manipulation of transfer prices, plays a more important role. Transfer prices are the prices at which branches of a given group buy their own products from one another. Within a single company, the branches in Bermuda sell services at a high price to entities located in the United States. Profits thus appear again in the tax havens and losses in the United States, in the large economies of continental Europe, and in Japan. In principle, intragroup transactions should be conducted using as a reference the market price of the goods and services traded, as if the subsidiaries were unrelated, what is known as "arm's-length pricing." But arm's-length pricing faces severe limitations. First, with billions of intragroup transactions every year, tax authorities cannot conceivably check that they are all correctly priced. And indeed there is compelling evidence of transfer mispricing by US firms.[30]

More fundamentally, in many cases the relevant reference prices simply do not exist. In 2003, less than a year before its initial public offering in August 2004, Google US transferred its search and advertisement technologies to "Google Holdings," a subsidiary incorporated in Ireland, but which for Irish tax purposes is a resident of Bermuda.[31] What was the fair-market value of Google's technologies at the time of transfer, before the Mountain View firm was even listed as a public company? Google US had an incentive to charge as little as possible for this transfer. We do not know whether it was able to do so: the transfer price is not public information. But journalistic leaks in the fall of 2014, "LuxLeaks," revealed that in many similar cases, the transfer prices that IT companies are able to charge when they send their intangibles to Bermuda is negligible, sometimes zero. Once that capital has arrived in Bermuda, all the profits that it generates are taxable there, where the corporate income tax rate is a modest 0%.

The issue is growing, as a rising number of international transactions within international divisions of a single company—such as the sale of proprietary trademarks, logos, and algorithms—are not replicated between third parties, hence have no reference price. Firms can sell themselves bananas or shovels at exorbitant prices—we've seen this—but the risk is high for companies that engage in such obvious fraud, as they can find themselves caught by the tax authorities. There is nothing less risky, by contrast, than manipulating the prices of patents, logos, labels, or algorithms, because the value of these assets is intrinsically difficult to establish. This is why the giants of tax avoidance are companies of the new economy: Google, Apple, and Microsoft. Taxing companies wanes to the same extent as immaterial capital gains in importance.

Tax Avoidance by US Firms: $130 Billion a Year

Quantifying the government revenue losses caused by profit shifting to lower-tax jurisdictions is not straightforward and, as with personal wealth, involves some margin of error. My approach relies on national accounts and balance-of-payments statistics, focusing on US firms.[32] Consider the basic macroeconomic aggregates of the US economy in 2013. Corporate profits (net of capital depreciation and interest payments) account for 14.5% of US national income, or $2.1 trillion. This figure includes $1.7 trillion of domestic profits, plus $650 billion of profits made by foreign firms owned by US residents (mostly subsidiaries of US corporations), minus $250 billion made by domestic firms owned by foreigners. Close to a third of US corporate profits (650/2,100), therefore, are made abroad.

Where do the $650 billion of foreign profits come from? The balance of payments provides a country-by-country decomposition of this total: according to the latest available figures, 55% is made in six low- or zero-tax countries: the Netherlands, Bermuda, Luxembourg, Ireland, Singapore, and Switzerland (fig. 8). Not much production or sale occurs in these offshore centers; very few workers are employed there—profits appear in Bermuda by sheer accounting manipulations. Since foreign profits account for a third of all US corporate profits, and tax havens for 55% of their foreign profits, the share of tax havens in total US corporate profits reaches 18% (55% of a third) in 2013. The use of tax havens by US firms has steadily increased since the 1980s and continues to rise.

By my estimate, the artificial shifting of profits to low-

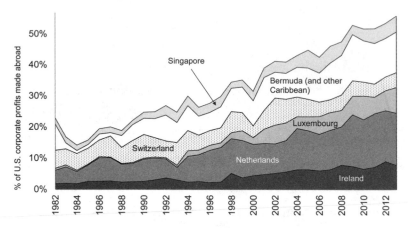

Figure 8: The share of tax havens in US corporate profits made abroad. Note: The figure charts the share of income on US direct investment abroad made in main tax havens. In 2013 total income on US direct investment abroad was about $500 billion, 17% coming from the Netherlands, 8% from Luxembourg, and so on.

Source: Gabriel Zucman, "Taxing Across Borders: Tracking Personal Wealth and Corporate Profits," *Journal of Economic Perspectives* 28, no. 4 (2014): 121–48.

tax locales enables US companies to reduce their tax liabilities, in total, by about $130 billion a year. Surveys of US multinationals conducted by the Bureau of Economic Analysis show that US firms pay a negligible 3% in taxes to foreign governments on the profits booked in the main low-tax jurisdictions displayed in figure 8. In the United States, contrary to what happens in most other countries, profits become taxable at a rate of 35% when they are repatriated (with a credit for all foreign corporate taxes previously paid). But in practice, there are few incentives to repatriate. The funds retained offshore can be used to purchase foreign companies, secure loans, pay foreign workers, and finance foreign investments, all of this without incurring US taxes. An even more extreme scenario is possible: firms that would like to use their accumulated earnings trapped offshore as they so wish can merge with foreign companies, in order to change their tax residence and avoid the US law, or what is known as a "tax inversion."

In 2004 Congress granted a repatriation tax holiday, letting multinationals bring their foreign profits back home if they paid a rate of 5.25%. The holiday failed to increase domestic employment, investment, or R&D;[33] it also boosted the foreign profits retained by US firms in tax havens. Today only a tiny fraction of the profits recorded by US firms in Bermuda and similar havens are brought back to the United States, and this share is falling with expectations of new holidays. In the end, not only do the profits made in the main havens bear negligible foreign taxes; they also mostly go untaxed by the Internal Revenue Service. Since they account for almost 20% of all US corporate profits, profit shifting to low-tax jurisdictions reduces the tax bill of US companies by close to 20%—or $130 billion annually.

The Decline in the Effective Corporate Tax Rate of US Firms

A direct consequence of the increased use of tax havens is that the effective tax rate paid by US firms is declining fast. The effective corporate tax rate is the ratio of all the corporate taxes paid by US firms (to US and foreign governments) by US corporate profits. Despite the fact that the nominal income tax rate in the United States has remained constant at 35%, the

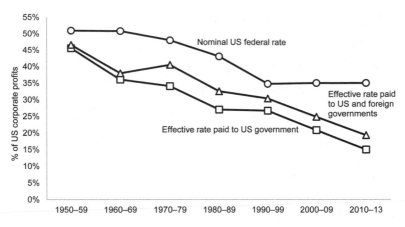

Figure 9: Nominal and effective corporate tax rates on US corporate profits. In 2013 of $100 of corporate profits earned by US residents, on average $16 is paid in corporate taxes to the US government (federal and state) and $4 to foreign governments.

Source: Gabriel Zucman, "Taxing Across Borders: Tracking Personal Wealth and Corporate Profits," *Journal of Economic Perspectives* 28, no. 4 (2014): 121–48.

effective rate has fallen from 30% in the late 1990s to barely 20% today (fig. 9).

Granted, not all that decline should be attributed to increased tax avoidance. Some changes in US laws have narrowed the tax base, like the introduction of a deduction of manufacturing income, or "bonus depreciation" during and in the aftermath of recessions; there is also a growing number of businesses in the United States, known as S-corporations, which are legally exempt from paying any corporate tax at all. But after factoring in all these changes, about two-thirds of the decline in the effective corporate tax rate since 1998 can be attributed to increased tax avoidance through low-tax jurisdictions.

The cost of tax avoidance by US firms is borne by both the United States and other countries' governments. Much of Google's profit that is shifted to Bermuda is earned in Europe; absent tax havens, Google would pay more taxes in France and Germany. On the other hand, some US corporations also use tax havens to avoid taxes on their US-source income. With national accounts data, it is hard to know which government loses most. In both cases, US shareholders win. Since equity ownership is very concentrated, even after including the equities owned by broad-based pension funds, so too are the benefits.

Accounting manipulations do not just cost governments a lot. They also cause basic macroeconomic statistics to lose significance, with adverse consequences for financial regulation and stability. The national accounts of Ireland, for example, are seriously contaminated by the trickery of multinationals. First, in the balance of payments: to shift their profits to the island, where they are taxed at only 12.5%, companies have their Irish branches import at low prices and export at artificially elevated prices—which results in an amazing trade surplus for Ireland of 25% of GDP! This surplus has nothing to do with any sort of competitive advantage; it doesn't benefit the Irish population at all: it is entirely paid back to the foreign owners of the firms that operate in Ireland, so that Irish national income is only 80% of Irish GDP. Manipulations of transfer prices then massively distort the share of each factor of production (capital and labor) in corporate value added: the artificially elevated profits booked by foreign-owned firms make the capital share rise to more than 50% in sectors where immaterial capital is large, as in the pharmaceutical industry.

A Twenty-First-Century Tax on Companies

What is to be done? The current approach of the OECD and G20 countries consists of trying to reform the existing system by strengthening transfer-pricing regulations.[34] The first efforts began in the second half of the 1990s, and yet the trend toward more widespread use of tax havens by US multinational companies has shown no particular sign of slowing down since then. The current approach, therefore, does not seem very promising. When it comes to manipulating transfer prices, companies will always be far ahead of the controllers, because their means are greater: the tax department of General Electric alone employs close to a thousand individuals. More resources granted to tax authorities might help curb tax avoidance. But in the United States, IRS funding is actually on a downward trend, and, besides, there is a real risk that increased spending by tax authorities would trigger even bigger corporate expenses, leading to no extra revenue and a true loss for the collectivity.

We need a radical reform of corporate taxation. A promising solution consists in starting from the global, consolidated profits of firms, which cannot be manipulated. To attribute profits to the different countries necessitates the use of an apportionment formula, perhaps some combination of sales, capital, and employment. For instance, if Starbucks makes half of its sales, has half of its capital and workers in the United States, then half of its profits would be taxable there. Ideally, the formula should be such that the location of profits cannot be manipulated. One way to achieve this is to attribute a substantial weight to the amount of sales made in each country, because companies have no control over that: they cannot move their customers from the United States to Bermuda! Once the profits are attributed to various countries, each remains free to tax them at the rate it wishes.

Even if the magical formula has not yet been invented (and probably doesn't exist), we can still understand the advantage of such a system: a tax that starts for the worldwide, consolidated profits of firms and apportion them to each country would render the manipulation of transfer prices meaningless. According to the estimates we have, we can thus expect an increase of 20% of the taxes paid by US (and probably other countries') companies. And multinationals themselves would save a lot of money, as they would no longer have to pay billions of dollars to find out how to make their profits appear in Ireland or Singapore while minimizing the legal risks. Only the firms specialized in tax optimization would lose in this; they would have to convert themselves into socially useful entities.

Is a tax on global profits utopian? Not at all. Comparable systems already exist on a regional level. This is how the state corporate taxes work in the United States: profits of US firms are calculated on a national level, then attributed to the different states using a formula that is difficult to manipulate—each state is then free to choose the rate at which it wishes to tax. The European Commission proposes an analogous solution for the EU, through its CCCTB (Common Consolidated Corporate Tax Base) project. Brussels has retained a simple apportionment formula, in which sales, salaries, and capital each count for a third. The Commission has had the good idea to exclude immaterial capital from its formula, to the great distress of consulting companies that specialize in optimization, and which thus see themselves deprived of their favorite pastime, the sending of patents, labels, and logos to offshore centers. The formula penalizes tax havens—where there are few sales, workers, or material capital—to the benefit of the large countries of continental Europe. The main problem is that at this stage the proposed plan is optional—each company may choose, if it wishes, to remain subject to the existing national taxes, whereas the plan should be made obligatory.

The United States and Europe will thus soon each have their own tax on companies that will function on a consolidated base, and not state by state. There is nothing unrealistic in envisioning their fusion. The EU and the United States are currently discussing the establishment of a zone of transatlantic free trade. The creation of a common base for the taxation of companies should appear at the top of the agenda in these negotiations. To prevent accounting manipulations and widespread avoidance, we must put fiscal questions at the center of trade policies.

There is no reason to wait: while the creation of a global financial register requires a high degree of cooperation, the United States and Europe can advance alone in reforming the taxation of companies. It is up to them to choose the way in which they wish to tax multinationals. An EU-US accord would build the foundation for a global base of taxation that would put an end to the large-scale shifting of profits to tax haven countries.

This book brings to light the concrete ways in which tax evasion by wealthy individuals and multinationals takes place. It calculates the cost for governments—that is, for us all—and above all proposes means to put an end to it.

Europe is in the midst of an interminable crisis. Many believe that they see in it the sign of an irreversible decline, but they are wrong. The Continent is the richest region in the world, and this is not going to change anytime soon. The private wealth there is greatly superior to the public debt. And, contrary to what we often believe, that wealth is taxable. The profits go to Bermuda, but the factories do not. The money hides in Switzerland, but it is not invested there. Capital does not move; it can simply be concealed. Europe is stealing from itself.

But this spiral can be reversed. Thanks to a global financial register, to an automatic exchange of information, and to a new way of taxing multinational companies, fiscal dissimulation can be stopped. Is this utopian? This is what most experts said of automatic exchange only five years ago, before rallying for it as a single voice. There are no technical obstacles to the measures I propose. The resistance from tax havens is not insurmountable, either: it can be broken by the threat of proportional trade sanctions.

Although solutions exist, governments have not been stellar up to now in their boldness or determination. It is thus high time to make them face up to their responsibilities. It is up to the citizens to mobilize, in Europe and perhaps above all in the tax havens. I don't believe that the majority of the inhabitants of Luxembourg—hardly 50% of which voted in the last elections—approve of the capture of the Grand Duchy by offshore finance. Nor do most Swiss accept the active aid that their bankers provide the billionaires who go there to avoid their fiscal obligations. To turn the page on large-scale fraud, the battle that must be fought is not just a battle between governments. It is above all a battle of citizens against the false inevitability of tax evasion and the impotence of nations.

1. These data are gathered on the website www.gabriel-zucman
.eu. This site provides details on all the calculations on which
the results presented in this book are based. Numbers, ta-
bles, graphs: all can be verified and reproduced to the letter.
This work is largely the result of four years of rigorous, but
certainly not definitive, research, which formed the basis of
my PhD dissertation: Gabriel Zucman, "Three Essays on the
World Distribution of Wealth" (PhD diss., Paris School of
Economics, EHESS, 2013). I thank in advance readers who
wish to send me their reactions, criticism, and suggestions to
improve my approach.

2. See Malik Mazbouri, *L'Émergence de la place financière suisse
(1890–1913)* (Lausanne: Antipodes, 2005).

3. Thomas Piketty and Gabriel Zucman, "Capital Is Back:
Wealth-Income Ratios in Rich Countries, 1700–2010," *Quarterly Journal of Economics* 129, no. 3 (2014).

4. "Keeping Mum," *Economist*, February 17, 1996, p. 90.

5. Sébastien Guex, "The Origin of the Swiss Banking Secrecy

Law and Its Repercussions for Swiss Federal Policy," *Business History Review* 74, no. 2 (2000).

6. Marc Perrenoud et al., *La place financière et les banques suisses à l'époque du national-socialisme: Les relations des grandes banques avec l'Allemagne (1931–1946)*, publication of the CIE, vol. 13 (Paris: Chronos/Payot, 2002), p. 98.

7. Janick Marina Schaufelbuehl, *La France et la Suisse ou la force du petit* (Paris: Presses de Sciences Po, 2009). On false certificates, see pp. 274–90 in particular.

8. Michael Findley, Daniel Nielson, and Jason Sharman, "Global Shell Games: Testing Money Launderers' and Terrorist Financiers' Access to Shell Companies," working paper, Centre for Governance and Public Policy, Griffith University, 2012, http://www.gfintegrity.org/wp-content/uploads/2014/05/Global-Shell-Games-2012.pdf.

9. Gabriel Zucman, "The Missing Wealth of Nations: Are Europe and the U.S. Net Debtors or Net Creditors?," *Quarterly Journal of Economics* 128, no. 3 (2013).

10. The estimate of $2.5 trillion includes $100 billion incorrectly recorded by the SNB as belonging to Switzerland. The exact figure could be much higher, on the order of several hundreds of billions of dollars.

11. All details are available online in the appendix to chapter 1 at www.gabriel-zucman.eu.

12. For a detailed description of my method, see Gabriel Zucman, "The Missing Wealth of Nations: Are Europe and the U.S. Net Debtors or Net Creditors?," *Quarterly Journal of Economics* 128, no. 3 (2013), and the online appendix at www.gabriel-zucman.eu.

13. Philip Lane and Gian Maria Milesi-Ferretti, "The External Wealth of Nations Mark II: Revised Estimates of Foreign Assets and Liabilities, 1970–2004," *Journal of International Economics* 73 (2007).

14. Ferdy Adam, "Impact de l'échange automatique d'informations en matière de produits financiers: Une tentative d'évaluation macro-économique appliquée au Luxembourg," Statec working paper no. 73, 2014.

15. James S. Henry, "The Price of Offshore Revisited: New Estimates for 'Missing' Global Private Wealth, Income, Inequality, and Lost Taxes," Tax Justice Network, July 2012, http://www.taxjustice.net/cms/upload/pdf/Price_of_Offshore_Revisited_120722.pdf.

16. Ruth Judson, "Crisis and Calm: Demand for U.S. Currency at Home and Abroad from the Fall of the Berlin Wall to 2011," IFDP working paper of the Board of Governors of the Federal Reserve System, November 2012, http://www.federalreserve.gov/pubs/ifdp/2012/1058/ifdp1058.pdf.

17. Adam, "Impact de l'échange automatique d'informations."

18. See, for instance, Credit Suisse, *Global Wealth Report 2013*, https://publications.credit-suisse.com/tasks/render/file/? fileID=BCDB1364-A105-0560-1332EC9100FF5C83.

19. Adam, "Impact de l'échange automatique d'informations," p. 8.

20. Thomas Piketty and Gabriel Zucman, "Capital Is Back: Wealth-Income Ratios in Rich Countries, 1700–2010," *Quarterly Journal of Economics* 129, no. 3 (2014).

21. *Bulletin de statistique et de législation comparée*, vol. 1, 1908, p. 280. See also the budget plan for 1910, *Bulletin de statistique et de législation comparée*, vol. 1, 1909, p. 627.

22. Niels Johannesen and Gabriel Zucman, "The End of Bank Secrecy?: An Evaluation of the G20 Tax Haven Crackdown," *American Economic Journal: Economic Policy 2014* 6, no. 1 (2014): 65–91, http://gabriel-zucman.eu/files/Johannesen Zucman2014.

23. See US Senate, *Offshore Tax Evasion: The Effort to Collect Unpaid Taxes on Billions in Hidden Offshore Accounts.* Staff Report of the Permanent Subcommittee on Investigations (Washington, DC: February 2014). See also Gabriel Zucman, "Taxing Across Borders: Tracking Personal Wealth and Corporate Profits," *Journal of Economic Perspectives* 28, no. 4 (2014): 121–48.

24. Federal administration of contributions, *Directives relatives à la fiscalité de l'épargne de l'UE (retenue d'impôt et déclaration volontaire)*, July 1, 2013, http://www.estv.admin.ch/.

25. Jean-Claude Juncker, quoted in "Le Luxembourg sera prêt à assouplir le secret bancaire en 2015," *Le Monde*, April 10, 2014, http://www.lemonde.fr/economie/article/2013/04/10/le-luxembourg-sera-pret-a-lever-le-secret-bancaire-en-2015_3157200_3234.html.

26. For a formal demonstration of these results, see Constantinos Syropoulos, "Optimum Tariffs and Retaliation Revisited: How Country Size Matters," *Review of Economic Studies* 69, no. 3 (2001).

27. On the commercialization of sovereignty, see Ronen Palan, "Tax Havens and the Commercialization of State Sovereignty," *International Organization* 56, no. (2002).

28. For some details, see the website of the Regulatory Oversight

Committee (ROC) of the Global Legal Entity Identifier System at http://www.leiroc.org.

29. Part of the material in this chapter was originally published in Gabriel Zucman, "Taxing Across Borders: Tracking Personal Wealth and Corporate Profits," *Journal of Economic Perspectives* 28, no. 4 (2014): 121–48.

30. Kimberly A. Clausing, "Tax-Motivated Transfer Pricing and US Intrafirm Trade Prices," *Journal of Public Economics* 87 (2003): 2207–23.

31. Jesse Drucker, "Google 2.4% Rate Shows How $60 Billion Is Lost to Tax Loopholes," *Bloomberg*, October 21, 2010, http://www.bloomberg.com/news/2010-10-21/google-2-4-rate-shows-how-60-billion-u-s-revenue-lost-to-tax-loopholes.html.

32. See Gabriel Zucman, "Taxing Across Borders: Tracking Personal Wealth and Corporate Profits," *Journal of Economic Perspectives* 28, no. 4 (2014): 121–48.

33. Dhammika Dharmapala, C. Fritz Foley, and Kristin J. Forbes, "Watch What I Do, Not What I Say: The Unintended Consequences of the Homeland Investment Act," *Journal of Finance* 66, no. 3 (2011): 753–87.

34. OECD, *Action Plan on Base Erosion and Profit Shifting*, July 2013, http://www.oecd.org/ctp/BEPSActionPlan.pdf.